GATHERED TO PRAY

PARISH LIFE SOURCEBOOKS

Barbara Hall, *Joining the Conversation*

Susan Coupland, *Beginning to Pray in Old Age*

GATHERED TO PRAY
Understanding Liturgical Prayer

A Parish Life Sourcebook

LOUIS WEIL

COWLEY PUBLICATIONS
FORWARD MOVEMENT

International Standard Book No.: 0-936384-35-2

Library of Congress Cataloging-in-Publication Data
Weil, Louis, 1935-
  Gathered to pray.

  (Parish life sourcebooks)
  Bibliography: p.
  1. Public worship. 2. Prayer. 3. Liturgics.
4. Episcopal Church. Book of common prayer (1979).
I. Title. II. Series.
BV15.W43   1986   264   86-17413
ISBN 0-936384-35-2 (pbk.)

Cowley Publications   Forward Movement
980 Memorial Drive   412 Sycamore Street
Cambridge, MA 02138   Cincinnati, OH 45202

to my mother

Acknowledgments

This book had its origin in a directed reading course. I want to express my gratitude to Curtis Almquist and Howard Marshall for their bibliographical work which was useful to me throughout the project. I am also grateful to Gerard Austin, Niels Rasmussen, and David Schlafer for suggestions along the way, and to Cynthia Shattuck, who pressed me to get the job done. Special thanks are due to Arliss Reul for her attentive care in the preparation of the manuscript for publication.

Quotations from the Book of Common Prayer are, unless otherwise indicated in the notes, taken from the contemporary forms in the 1979 BCP.

Excerpts from the English translation of *The Roman Missal*, copyright 1973, International Commission on English in the Liturgy, Inc. All rights reserved.

Louis Weil
Nashotah House

Pentecost 1986

Cowley Publications is a work of the Society of St. John the Evangelist, a religious community for men in the Episcopal Church. The books we publish are a significant part of our ministry, together with the work of preaching, spiritual direction, and hospitality. Our aim is to provide books that will enrich their readers' religious experience and challenge it with fresh approaches to religious concerns.

Series Introduction

Parish Life Sourcebooks is a new series of books which address issues arising in the parish for lay persons as well as clergy. Sourcebooks from Cowley Publications not only suggest solutions to parish problems, they also create imaginative alternatives to traditionally accepted ways of thinking about a particular issue. Such issues — from new concepts in Bible study and issuing sacraments to children to the concerns of becoming a eucharistic parish — have a wide-ranging impact throughout the parish, and are the sort of questions that emerge at coffee hours where clergy and laity informally grapple with theological concerns.

Parish Life Sourcebooks are working documents designed to assist in these theological conversations. On the one hand each provides a presentation of an essential parish issue, covering the basic information needed for a full discussion; on the other, Cowley Sourcebooks serve as a springboard for dialogue, encouraging readers to go beyond the book itself to create their own interpretations of the issues and search for their own conclusions. Through wide margins, ample end pages, and helpful bibliographies, Sourcebooks lend themselves to the complete use of the reader, becoming, if used to their full potential, that reader's own creation.

Parish Life Sourcebooks assist each parish community, regardless of affiliation or denomination, in the effort to bring together clergy and laity on key issues that they face on a daily basis. In so far as Sourcebooks encourage healthy discussion on topics we do not often speak about, but on which we always have an opinion, we welcome them into the theological arena of our time.

The Society of St. John the Evangelist is continuing to produce for the Church attractive, intelligently prepared books that are consistent with the tradition of Cowley and related to the contemporary parish scene. They are, in my judgment, among the finest publications available for the Church at large. I am very happy to commend them to clergy and lay persons. They will provide interesting and stimulating materials for further theological reflection and prayer leading to a deeper and richer commitment to the Christian Gospel.

John B. Coburn

Contents

Chapter One

On Liturgical Prayer

There seems never to be a shortage of publications on prayer. They come in every size, from pamphlet to lengthy tome, offering a constant stream of advice to those who want somehow to pray more effectively than they feel they do. Many readers of such materials may have shared a common frustration with me: although we may have spent a great deal of time and energy reading *about* prayer, prayer itself often remains on the surface of our experience.

The quantity of publications on prayer has been matched in recent years by a formidable array of material on the liturgy, both technical studies on the history and theology of the liturgy, and more popular writings on the pastoral dimensions of liturgical worship. The liturgical

[1]

movement and its confirmation in the *Constitution on the Sacred Liturgy* of Vatican II have contributed to significant reforms in the liturgical rites of the major Christian communions during the past two decades. There has also been a growing emphasis in theological education on the significance of the liturgy for all aspects of the Christian life.

It is striking, however, that most publications on prayer speak from the perspective of the individual at prayer, that is, of the particularities and problems of private prayer. On the whole, there is little substantial attention given to corporate worship as the primary focus of Christian prayer. In many cases, one might easily conclude that prayer is essentially a private activity, and that liturgical worship is merely a ritual occasion at which a sermon is preached and prescribed ceremonial is performed. If that were all liturgical worship involves, it could be referred to as "prayer" merely by way of convention, and true prayer would be limited to an activity done in solitude. This view would confirm Alfred North Whitehead's dictum that religion is what people do with their solitude.

If we consider our heritage within the Judeo-Christian tradition, however, this radical distinction between private prayer and public worship cannot be maintained, and we find rather two types of prayer, distinct yet complementary, and both fundamental to the life of faith. The psalms offer us a repertory of prayers which are sometimes corporate, sometimes individual, and in still other examples a fusion of the two. Psalm 44, for example, is a communal lament, the collective voice of a people praying to God in evil times:

[2]

Every day we gloried in God,
  and we will praise your Name for ever.
Nevertheless, you have rejected and humbled us
  and do not go forth with our armies.
You have made us fall back before our adversary,
  and our enemies have plundered us.
You have made us like sheep to be eaten
  and have scattered us among the nations.

  (44:8-11)

These words are clearly the cry of a community, the expression of their common distress.

If we look at Psalm 44 as a whole, we find that its essential thrust lies within this corporate dimension of prayer. The psalm begins with an acclamation of God's mighty acts in history by which a people was created:

We have heard with our ears, O God,
  our forefathers have told us, the deeds you
    did in their days, in the days of old.
How with your hand you drove the peoples out
  and planted our forefathers in the land;
    how you destroyed nations and made
        your people flourish.
For they did not take the land by their sword,
  nor did their arm win the victory for them;
    but your right hand, your arm, and the
        light of your countenance,
  because you favored them.

  (44:1-3)

[3]

Yet even within this essentially corporate framework, the psalm reveals the interplay of the individual with the communal, the "I" and the "we":

> You are my King and my God;
>   you command victories for Jacob.
> Through you we pushed back our adversaries;
>   through your Name we trampled on those who
>   rose up against us.
> For I do not rely on my bow,
>   and my sword does not give me the victory.
> Surely, you gave us victory over our adversaries
>   and put those who hate us to shame.

(44:4-7)

Furthermore, the complementarity of the communal and the individual dimensions of prayer is dramatically expressed in the series of laments with the following juxtaposition:

> You have made us a byword among the nations,
>   a laughing-stock among the peoples.
> My humiliation is daily before me,
>   and shame has covered my face . . . .

(44:14-15)

In this psalm, the individual is seen in a radical identification with the community. What God has done to form a people touches each individual's life; the anguish of the individual is a particular mirror of the anguish of the people as they seek to understand the will of God in the experience of defeat.

This sense of the individual in relation to the community, and similarly of individual prayer in relation to corporate prayer, is fundamental in Judaism for the idea of "the people of God," which is in turn the root image of the Church in Christianity. To a great extent, books on prayer have not given adequate attention to this *ecclesial* dimension of prayer, the fact that prayer in community is the starting point for a pattern of prayer which is characteristically Christian. For baptism, our incorporation in Christ, is incorporation into the *ecclesia orans*, the praying Church. Similarly, in many books on the liturgy, various aspects of liturgical development are explored without a clear indication that liturgy is in the first place *prayer*, corporate prayer, the prayer of the Church gathered in faith to offer praise and thanksgiving to God.

The understanding that liturgical rites are a primary form of prayer cannot be taken for granted. The liturgical norms of too many parish churches are a potent sign to the contrary. The pattern of liturgy experienced by countless Christians week after week is rather like a liturgical drill, smoothly or sloppily executed, a highly predictable routine which includes the traditional materials of public prayer (Scripture, hymns, sacramental forms), but which is celebrated in a style which inhibits their realization as corporate prayer. This deprived style is often a matter of attitude on the part of both clergy and laity: a domination of the liturgical action by the clergy and a consequent failure to foster diversity of roles, an excessive speed or virtually mechanical approach to the texts, and the assumption of second-class or passive status on the part of the laity. All of these contribute to an impoverishment of the experience of the liturgy as common prayer. If liturgical renewal has helped us to recover the sense that liturgy is what the Church does when it assembles, our pastoral implementation of that insight has often failed to make some important connections clear.

For many Christians, therefore, both laity and clergy, "true" prayer is experienced and conceived as a private activity, or perhaps as a small group experience. In these contexts, the personal dimensions of prayer are more immediately accessible, whereas the routinized celebration of the rites tends to obscure or even overwhelm the sense of a connectedness between ordinary living and corporate worship. A recurring lament has been voiced in recent years that even people who go regularly to Sunday worship do not sense its relevance to their daily lives. When this situation exists, there are two frequent and unfortunate results. Those who hunger for the affective and personal expressions of Christian faith look to private or group prayer for what formal liturgy has failed to supply. For others, the ritual routine offers a convenient way to encapsulate religious expression, and to compartmentalize religious concerns into a Sunday morning routine. Often, perhaps unconsciously, this latter result signifies that worship is regarded as an act apart, even an escape, from the realities of daily life. This is a strange understanding of worship for a faith based upon the Incarnation, in which human reality is proclaimed as the field of God's action. In both cases, the liturgical model being responded to is only a shadow of what liturgical prayer is called to be in the life of the Church. The tragedy is that inadequate liturgical formation and experience has created a fabric of distorted expectations as to what liturgy is.

Authentic liturgical prayer always involves a mysterious mingling of universal and particular elements. The universal dimension grows out of the relation of the local community to the whole Church, whereby the liturgy of the local church is part of the much vaster landscape of the Church's worship at all times and in all places. The tradition of shared liturgical forms is a basic sign of the unity of faith and prayer of the Church both throughout the world and across history. For many Christians, a sense of the Church beyond the parish or even diocesan boundaries is linked to a sensitively prepared "prayer of the people" in which the assembly is called to pray for concerns from all parts of the world, and not merely from a narrowly congregational focus. A variety of publications, such as the Anglican Cycle of Prayer, call the local churches to an organized pattern of prayer and concern for the Church all over the world. Such prayer should be linked to active response when there are needs abroad to which local communities might respond in material ways.

The liturgy offers signs of our unity not only with the Church throughout the world, but also the Church of past and future generations. Each celebration in the proclamation of the readings from Scripture holds before the gathered community the history of God's saving deeds, what is often referred to as "salvation history." No single liturgical rite is isolated in meaning from the unfolding of God's purposes in human history. This is why the reading of Scripture is a fundamental dynamic of the liturgical tradition and a sign of the unity of all believers across time. It is the proclamation of the Word of God which proclaims and reminds us again and again of God's mighty acts within which we, too, find our place as members of the people of God.

A further dimension of this unity across history is found in the persistence of a fundamental shape to Christian liturgical prayer, a continuity of structure which, in spite of cultural adornments and modifications, gives us a unity of purpose in our liturgical assemblies with Christians throughout the centuries. A certain conservatism in the evolution of the liturgy means that even particular forms of prayer (many of the collects, for example, have been prayed by the Church for centuries) have undergone translation and refinement as needed, yet remain a powerful example of continuity between the Church today and in past generations.

Particular or local aspects of the liturgy reflect the life situation of the community, its experiences and needs, its cultural identity, and the distinctive gifts of its members. This means that the universal aspects of the liturgical tradition must be vivified in the particularities of the local assembly. A community which lives near the sea, for example, will have a special sensitivity for related images in Scripture, and will often celebrate events which would be irrelevant to inland communities, such as the blessing of fishing boats. A community which does not speak the dominant language of the country in which it lives, and is also a gathering of people who have a strong ethnic identity, will incorporate music and crafts which give expression to that identity. In more ordinary ways, the fact that certain members of a church have particular gifts which may be incorporated into their public worship, means that the local celebration will always bear the print of the local community as it celebrates a ritual pattern shared with Christians all over the world. If these local gifts are overlooked for the sake of conformity to a rigid model, the liturgy risks a disconnectedness from the realities of the lives of worshippers. Yet if corporate prayer is generated entirely from within the local community, however, worship as the sign of a common faith — which the liturgical tradition offers and which is the common heritage of all Christians — can be seriously undermined. The Church is not merely an amalgam of disconnected congregations; it is the one Body of Christ.

On the other hand, if the universal dimension is given absolute dominance, the liturgy may come to be understood as only the repetition of ancient rites. In this perspective, change and adaptation in the liturgy are anathema because the printed text is accorded an inordinate importance. The value of the universal dimension as an expression of the unity and continuity of the Church is most effectively realized when there is a sensitive integration of the distinctive gifts of the local community into its liturgical celebrations. Universal and particular dimensions are thus experienced as complementary: the local church finds its voice within the framework of the great tradition of the Church's common prayer in every time and place.

*   *   *   *

On Liturgical Prayer

To approach the meaning of liturgical prayer from this perspective is to affirm what I earlier identified as the *ecclesial* foundation of Christian prayer. To speak of prayer as ecclesial is to say that it is the articulation of faith: trust in the God who is the source of all that is, and whose activity in human history is realized with a unique intensity in the Incarnation of Jesus Christ, and who continues to give life and to sustain all things through the Holy Spirit. Trust in that God calls for response. Faith leads to prayer. The whole tradition of liturgical prayer is the Church's instrument for holding up the wonder of God's activity in a context of praise and thanksgiving. All aspects of the Church's life, in worship or in service, are expressions of faith, are ways in which faith is articulated in visible form. All Christian activity presumes faith, a turning toward and acknowledgment of the God who is. The sacramental life signifies and sustains that turning and commitment. Christian initiation incorporates individuals into the Body of the Risen Lord. The culmination of the process of incorporation is communion, the shared sign of the living presence of Christ in the community of faith which proclaims him as Lord. Authentic communion can never be an act of private piety because it is essentially an action of the whole Body. Private eucharistic devotion is a contradiction in terms, because the eucharist always celebrates and reconstitutes the unity of Christians in Christ. The energy which animates all liturgical prayer is the activity of the Holy Spirit, who nourishes our faith in the paschal mystery into which we have been grafted through baptism.

Faith is the fundamental gift, not as a private bridge between the individual and God, but as the disposition of the Church, its way of being in regard to God. Without this foundation of faith, all prayer, whether liturgical or not, is vain. Acts of devotion, whether public or private, do not create faith, nor can they serve as a substitute for it. The importance of our acts of prayer lies in their dignity as instruments of faith, the ways in which faith is articulated. This articulation involves words only in a secondary sense, for in the first instance prayer is neither formal nor spontaneous words, but rather the disposing of self, in community or in solitude, before the Holy One.

For any adequate analysis of liturgical prayer, we must recognize that prayer does not require any external elements. A common criticism leveled by the Puritans against the Book of Common Prayer in the sixteenth and seventeenth centuries was that the book was filled with "the inventions of men," that is, with non-biblical patterns of formal prayer that suffocated the true spirit of prayer which the Holy Spirit inspired in the spontaneous utterance of the heart. The danger always exists that liturgical prayer may be understood merely as the repetition of printed texts. Yet many contemporary Christians who have shared in the charismatic movement, or simply in small group prayer, have come to realize that spontaneous prayer can also distintegrate into the repetition of set formulas. Insistence upon "free" prayer is no assured solution to this problem. In the most radical sense, prayer is not a matter of words at all.

Authentic prayer grows out of a deep interior silence, a still point at which faith looks in love and hope to the One upon whom faith rests. It is not only for the individual that such silence is imperative for authentic prayer; it is essential for the community's prayer as well. Silence is at the heart of corporate prayer. Because our human nature communicates meaning through articulated sounds, this silence will overflow into some form, and such forms will usually involve words. It is precisely to facilitate the shared articulation of this silent, faithful disposition that liturgical forms are significant for the corporate life of the Church. Yet for centuries the Church has been plagued by an essentially externalized understanding of liturgical worship. Liturgical prayer has often become associated with a performance mentality, in which authorized texts and prescribed rites are given priority, and their articulation is restricted to qualified personnel, more particularly to the ordained clergy.[1]

In the light of this development, one can see the integrity of the Quaker movement, both in its anti-clericalism and in its insistence upon the primacy of shared silence, as the foundation for the assembly's worship. The liturgical churches need to hear the judgment which the Quaker tradition brings upon a merely externalized understanding of liturgical prayer. Recent decades have seen a recovery of our sense that the whole community of faith participates in liturgical prayer. Clerical domination of the liturgical rites is gradually giving way to patterns of liturgical ministries which manifest the diversity of the Church's corporate life. The ordained continue to exercise a pastoral stewardship in the liturgy as a service to the whole community, but that service is increasingly understood as complementary to and supportive of the assembly's legitimate role.

Yet the excessive formalization of liturgical rites, albeit in a variety of styles, continues to shape the liturgical experience of the majority of regular worshippers. In many parishes around the country, evidence suggests that liturgical renewal has dealt primarily with external aspects of liturgical change, such as ritual and textual adjustments exemplified in the 1979 Book of Common Prayer, and with a certain simplification and reshaping of the style in which those rites are celebrated. To the degree that this observation is correct, there remains the far more significant frontier of liturgical formation, namely, the recovery of an ecclesial sense of faith and ministry which will form from within the community the specific pattern of external celebration. Given the formative impact of experience, our inherited expectations have shaped the Church as a whole for the type of clericalized model I discussed earlier. A kind of revolution of the liturgical sense is needed, and this cannot emerge overnight. The basis for such a revolution lies in the wider implications of a restored adult catechumenate, a program of adult formation whose goal is Christian maturity and enablement for ministry. Such a revolution in our expectations for lay participation in the Church's life will inevitably lead to a remolding of the models of liturgical celebration in which that life is proclaimed.

The liturgy is always an articulation of the Church's faith. Corporate worship must be understood and experienced as inseparable from its underlying energies if it is not to disintegrate into a merely external routine. The liturgy proclaims through word and action the signs of redemption, and is thus a constant renewal of the baptismal covenant for all Christians as they participate in the celebration of that faith. It holds the Gospel in its fullness before the gathered community, calling people to repentance, to a renewal and deepening of faith, and to a common thanksgiving for the gifts of grace. If such a recovery is to be fully realized, the catechetical formation of all Christians must enable them to make connections between their most deeply interior selves and the Church's corporate prayer. This is a critical test for any pattern of Christian formation. It is the whole of our personal life that we bring into corporate worship, or else we court a kind of liturgical schizophrenia.

In other words, external liturgical reform, such as the revision of the official books, has created a framework in which the corporate prayer of faith may take place, but it does not automatically assure that such prayer is taking place. By and large, we have been formed to take the expectations of private prayer with us into the corporate assembly. Is it any surprise that for many Christians new rites which invade their privacy are seen as an intrusion upon their purpose in going to church? The difficulty experienced when the Kiss of Peace was restored to its place in the liturgy is an excellent case in point. If we go to church in order to nurture individual piety, then such an act of community is painfully disruptive of our reason for being there. But if liturgical praying is different from private praying, then a new set of expectations must be formed in the members of the community. The formation of such corporate expectations should be a primary goal of Christian education.

Although liturgical prayer is a different type of prayer from prayer in private or in a small group, it does not abolish the importance of these other forms of prayer. Yet it is inappropriate to criticize liturgical prayer for failing to fulfill the expectations associated with other types of prayer. There is, in fact, a deep complementarity between different modes of prayer which becomes evident as we experience each in its integrity; but the two are not the same. The ritual prayer in which we participate when we gather for the liturgy is the essential act of Christian memory, in which the baptized community is reminded through Scripture, the homily, and the sacramental action of the groundplan of redemption. The liturgy lifts up within our human experience the common history which all Christians share and invites us to take our place in that story of salvation.

It is possible that our alienation from genuinely corporate prayer is linked to an evident lack of ease with prayer in the daily pattern of our lives both as individuals and in our families. The general disappearance of prayer in families has been widely commented upon. Even in the homes of Christians who attend church regularly, prayer is often limited to a blessing before a meal, and that in many cases in a perfunctory form or else sentimentalized as it is "performed" by a small child. Such situations point to a loss of the naturalness of Christian prayer. So we go to church on Sundays hoping that the liturgy will fill the emptiness we feel through the absence of daily prayer from our lives, both as individuals and as members of a family. But we are disappointed there as well, and the emptiness of the one exacerbates the ineffectiveness of the other in a self-perpetuating vicious circle. The often-heard cry of the laity of their desire to be taught how to pray is indicative of the Church's failure to prepare Christians for an activity which they are asked not only to share with others each Sunday, but to practice in their homes throughout the week as well. Ignoring this spiritual bankruptcy will not make the problem go away. Prayer, whether corporate or individual, requires grounding, a vigorous ministry of mature formation in faith. Otherwise people are left merely with "saying prayers," which is a superficial manifestation of the reality.

The complementarity between liturgical prayer and private prayer emerges as we recognize in the most familiar texts of the liturgical tradition a splendid resource for private prayer. The interweaving of our spontaneous prayer with such a fundamental text as

> Holy, holy, holy Lord, God of power and might,
> heaven and earth are full of your glory

immediately unites our private prayer with the prayer of the Church in heaven and on earth. We have long experienced that connection preeminently in our use of the Lord's Prayer in both liturgical and private prayer, but we have not generally seen in this use a model for the interplay between the Church's common voice of prayer and our particular acts of faith and devotion. When we repeat such familiar forms week after week at the eucharist, is it the style of our Sunday worship that inhibits our making this connection, or is it simply that the usual patterns of Christian formation do not develop such awareness? Both the experience of praying with the Church, and also the catechetical formation, are needed to enable believers to connect corporate prayer with their own deeply interior places where faith must find articulation. There is growing evidence from Christians who practice this interweaving of liturgical texts with private and spontaneous prayer that such interweaving creates a strong bridge between the two. This bridge fosters identification of the intensity of private affective devotion with an authentic experience of corporate liturgical prayer.[2] This is quite a different basis upon which to integrate the various modes of prayer than is the attempt to approach corporate prayer with the expectation that it will fill the void left by an absence of private prayer from daily life.

In a useful survey of the patterns of prayer practiced in the early Church, Balthasar Fischer has lamented the lack of attention which recent liturgical research has given to the devotional practices of Christian families and individuals in the patristic period and in the middle ages. Fischer asserts that the home was the birthplace of common prayer. He writes,

> The most important characteristic of common prayer in the ancient Christian family seems to me to lie in the extension, into the home, of public worship . . . . [The Church had not come] to the painful dichotomy that is the hall-mark of the medieval domestic piety, which is obliged to set up a second universe of prayer — easily understood, and so more primitive, more subjective — side by side with the liturgy, since the latter was now incomprehensible and dominated by the clergy.[3]

[17]

Here Fischer is pointing to what is almost certainly the fundamental cause of the alienation of the Church as a whole from the true spirit of corporate liturgical prayer: clericalization. Although it does not lie within the scope of this book to discuss fully the impact of clericalism upon liturgical worship, it is at least important to affirm the implications of Fischer's insight. The progressive domination of public worship by the clergy is paralleled by the emergence of a private world of lay piety cut off from the cleansing lifestream of the Church's corporate prayer. The victims of this development were not only the laity but also the clergy, whose role in the Church's life came more and more to be seen as set apart from the ordinary lives of Christians. Although it shifted its focus from sacrament to word, even the Reformation was not able to deal effectively with the general mindset which clericalism created. In a variety of ways, the Church today is coming to deal with a necessary reversal of the effects of clericalization upon the Church's experience of corporate worship.[4]

If we look at the weekly assembly as the corporate focus to which all the diverse members of the Christian community bring the particularities of their daily lives, the Sunday eucharist appears as a collection-point, a place at which there is a gathering of the whole. The liturgical rite creates a common ground of the community's corporate identity in Christ.

The local assembly is a kind of icon of the Church, the gathering of the baptized people of God. During the week, we have suggested, the great texts of the liturgical tradition can flow over into the family and private devotions of individual Christians and form a bridge leading back to the assembly gathered on Sunday, where the liturgy will *collect* all the particularities of life and ministry and prayer which have filled the weekdays of the members. This is not merely a play on words: to see the Sunday eucharist as a collection-point is to gain a profound insight into the corporate nature of the rite as a whole. This link, Balthasar Fischer has suggested, was characteristic of the common prayer of the early Church, and it sets a standard for us in the renewal of liturgical worship in our own time.

Through our baptism into the paschal mystery of Christ, Christians are committed to a way of living, a life of prayerful response. The foundations of that life are thanksgiving to God the Father, as the source of all that exists; identification with Christ, who in the Incarnation has identified his divinity with our humanity in such a way that we may become Christ to others; and consecrated self-offering through the presence of the Holy Spirit to lead us and to sustain us. This Trinitarian groundplan of the Christian life is expressed in many ways and regularly renewed in the corporate worship of the Body. Christian liturgical prayer is itself the outward manifestation of this interior faith. In the eucharistic action, Trinitarian faith finds its richest expression in the proclamation of the Great Thanksgiving. That faith, however, flows over into all facets of both corporate worship and private prayer.

The collect as a form of prayer is a kind of microcosm of this Trinitarian faith. The role of the collect in the liturgy is to focus the attention of the gathered community on a particular aspect of the mystery of faith. It is thus a model for the complementary dimensions of unity and diversity in Christian prayer. As we examine the history of the collect, its content and its theology, we shall find it to be a model in miniature of the fundamental energies of liturgical prayer. Perhaps the frustration which many Christians have experienced in regard to growth in the life of prayer will be diminished as we recover a sense of the essential relation between daily forms of prayer and the corporate prayer of the Church on the Lord's Day.

> Almighty and everlasting God, you have given to us your servants grace, by the confession of a true faith, to acknowledge the glory of the eternal Trinity, and in the power of your divine Majesty to worship the Unity: Keep us steadfast in this faith and worship, and bring us at last to see you in your one and eternal glory, O Father; who with the Son and the Holy Spirit live and reign, one God, for ever and ever. *Amen.*

(Collect for Trinity Sunday)

Chapter Two

The Collect is Corporate Prayer

The Holy Eucharist, which the Book of Common Prayer calls the principal act of Christian worship on the Lord's Day, is often experienced as a kind of liturgical routine. Even laity who attend church regularly will admit that they do not understand the basic sense of the rites in which they participate each week. This does not mean that they are left untouched by this experience, as if the liturgy were merely an external drill, for effective ritual has an amazing power to speak to us of the Holy One at levels of our being that lie far deeper than those of rational understanding. But as stewards of these rites the clergy are often content to reproduce a familiar model week after week, and to ignore the terrifying pastoral reality that for many of the people in the pews there is little awareness of what this all means.

A significant part of the problem is that we have inherited, laity and clergy alike, a view that the liturgy is entirely the business of the priest as to deciding what will or will not be done. That view is even supported by the canons which set the guidelines of the Church's life, where it is stipulated that "the control of the worship and the spiritual jurisdiction of the Parish, are vested in the Rector."[1] The use of the words *control* and *jurisdiction* in this context is a significant indication of a common approach toward liturgical responsibility. This control of the liturgy by the clergy is a holdover of the clericalism of the middle ages, in which all aspects of the Church's faith and practice were subject to the authority of the hierarchy. Nor was this clericalism adequately confronted at the time of the Reformation. It is an entrenched attitude not only among many of the ordained, but even among laity who are content to accept a kind of second-class status that allows them the ease of a passive role in the Church's life.

This active/passive distinction has far-reaching implications in all dimensions of the Christian life, but its practical expression in public worship bears an especially bitter fruit. The New Testament holds up a model of the Church whose members are endowed with a wide range of gifts for ministry. It is this model which most adequately sets the context in which to consider the specific nature of the ordained ministries as complemented by the other gifts of the Christian community. Public worship is a mirror of the Church's self-understanding as a community of faith with widely diverse gifts among its members, who yet find their fundamental unity in a common act of praise.

Ordination quite appropriately involves a special responsibility for word and sacrament in the Church. The candidate for ordination to the priesthood is asked in the Examination,

> Will you endeavor so to minister the Word of God and the sacraments of the New Covenant, that the reconciling love of Christ may be known and received?

In the Prayer of Consecration which follows, the bishop prays that the ordinand may "boldly proclaim the gospel of salvation; and rightly administer the sacraments of the New Covenant." Responsibility, however, is not the same as autocracy, and the liturgy continues to be an area about which many clergy are defensively protective. Yet their legitimate role in liturgical leadership must be rooted in a clear sense of the essential nature of liturgical prayer as a common action of the whole people of God.

The liturgical leadership of the clergy is expressed in the development of a model of liturgical worship which is genuinely corporate, and in which the active participation of all who are gathered is the anticipated norm. For that, there is a great need for a more thorough liturgical formation than seems to find a place in our programs of adult education. As a seminary teacher, I have an opportunity each year to assess the situation as a new group of students arrives, coming to us from parishes and missions all over the country. Due to a general lack of grounding in the nature of the liturgy, I have found it impossible to begin the liturgical program in those areas of history and theology in which the candidates will require specialized knowledge for pastoral ministry. As a result, the first course in liturgy is an introduction to basic matters which I feel should be part of the formation of all committed laity, not just those who intend to be ordained.

The absence of such formation and instruction is the key to the situation noted at the beginning of this chapter, that is, the general lack of understanding on the part of the laity of the rites in which they regularly participate. This issue is directly related to the subject of this book because the gathering of God's people to pray *together* is fostered by the liturgical structure itself. That structure is an instrument which, when properly understood and implemented, supports the liturgical action as corporate prayer, the common prayer of a people who share a common faith.

In programs with laity, I have found again and again that the clergy often take too much for granted, as in their casual use of Latin liturgical terms, or in their assumption that the development of liturgical understanding among the laity is accomplished simply by attending services. This latter view might seem to be supported by my earlier comment about the power of ritual to manifest the holy, but history shows that a rite tends to accumulate divergent elements which can in the end undermine and obscure the fundamental meaning of the rite itself. One has only to remember that medieval Christianity tolerated non-communion as a standard of lay participation in the eucharist for several centuries to realize how external factors may be allowed to shape a practice which contradicts the basic meaning of a rite.[2] The influence of a scientific world view has tended to create a society that is ill at ease with the languages of the imagination: symbol and gesture, the body in ritual movement, the truths which only poetry can express. Yet these are the languages of the liturgy, and the Church's ministry of formation in Christ requires an introduction to that world and its way of expressing ultimate meaning.[3]

The essential structure of a liturgical rite is very simple. The gathering community brings to that common action all the richness of its own culture and the particularity of individual gifts. It is this human dimension which fleshes out the basic structure and in which the non-verbal elements have so important a role to play. There is an underlying sense to the structure which manifests the relation of the liturgical act to the being of the Church. Do people realize that the first liturgical element is the gathering itself, the assembly as God's people in this place? It seems that the individualization of religious practice which is characteristic of our world works in opposition to the first intention of the liturgy. It is naive to assume that the attitudes of our culture, which work upon all of us in often subtle ways, can be discarded simply by entering the church building. If the language of the liturgy is to be understood and shared, then its language, and the world of meaning to which that language points, must become a priority in Christian formation. This means that the clergy must understand the liturgy as more than the performance of rubrics, a kind of liturgical drill, and must themselves discover it as the dance of eternal life, not a solo dance for the clergy, but a ritual dance in which all are participants.

This approach will seem rather remote from the familiar patterns of liturgical worship in our parish churches, yet in most places, at least some of the time, something of this vision of the liturgy breaks through. It may come with the singing of a favorite hymn, when suddenly a gathering of individuals will find itself transformed into a community by the experience of shared song. An effective reading of Scripture can create a renewed awareness of ourselves as the Church, and certainly this is one of the goals of preaching. Or this vision may come in unexpected ways which call us out of our private worlds into the common world of faith. However it may occur, the nature of the liturgy as corporate prayer constantly summons us, if we are alert to its language, to a sense of our unity in Christ.

What has all of this to do with the subject of this chapter, the collect? Too often, in liturgical manuals, collects are discussed only in terms of their form as a stylized pattern of prayer. I will consider them in that light, but I have felt it important to begin with a wider framework. If we do not perceive the basic intention of the liturgical act, we shall easily miss the wider implications of the collect in relation to the corporate prayer of those who gather. The history of the collect reveals it to be a sign of the *gathering* character of liturgical worship, but, unfortunately, a sign whose basic intent has gradually been obscured as a sense of the liturgical act has been lost.

Our attempt to define a collect must, therefore, be more than a reiteration of its standard elements. In this chapter we shall explore the origins of the collect as a form of prayer within the liturgy and then later consider its place in the overall structure of the rites. This will require attention to the role of silence in the liturgy, which provides an opportunity for the offering of individual petitions in silent prayer by the people assembled. It is these petitions which are then summed up in the general and inclusive language of the collect-form, and which are thus a key to its own structure. As we survey these issues, the collect will emerge as a far more significant moment within the rhythm of the liturgy than we have usually experienced: it is the point at which the private concerns of individual Christians are linked specifically to the common concerns of the whole Church.

*   *   *   *

Although the term "collect" is often used indiscriminately in reference to any three-part prayer (involving an address to God, a petition, and a doxology), the word points historically to a more precise set of associations. In other words, the customary three-part structure of the collect is only one dimension of its character. As I said earlier, the first basic element of the liturgy is the gathering of the people for an act of common worship — what is usually referred to as the entrance rite.

On great occasions that gathering rite may be very complex, involving a rich array of musical material. On more typical occasions, all that may be required to initiate a sense of corporate or common prayer may be an opening hymn. At a small gathering on an early weekday morning, this first ritual act may be very much simplified, as the rubrics of the Book of Common Prayer permit. Yet in all these instances, as divergent in style as they may be, the collect is always present. In this we see a hint of the relation of the collect to the intention of the entrance rite, that is, to draw a disparate group of individuals into a common act of worship. The collect concludes the entrance rite by drawing the assembly into a shared offering of petitionary prayer, where all their individual concerns are summed up in a prayer which unites these diverse people in their common prayer as the Body of Christ.

Whereas the Roman rite has referred to the prayer which concludes the introductory rite of the eucharist simply as *oratio* ("prayer"), the Anglican tradition has followed the northern European custom which referred to this prayer as *collectio* ("collect"). In medieval Gaul, the bishop or priest who presided at either the eucharist or the divine office would use a *collectio*, a short formula of prayer, to sum up or to conclude the prayer of those who were assembled. The term was never used in this way in the earliest Roman liturgical books, but a similar term — *collecta* — does appear, used in reference to a gathering or assembly of the faithful, but not with regard to any specific formula of prayer.

It is easy to see how these two originally distinct yet similar terms might fuse, as Roman liturgical documents were copied and propagated throughout northern Europe as part of the policy of the Emperor Charlemagne. The emperor saw in the Roman rite a basis for religious unity and conformity for his empire. But as the Roman documents were copied, Gallican elements were gradually inserted into the Roman liturgical materials.[4] Thus the Roman term *collecta* replaced the Gallican term *collectio*, but with the sense which the latter term had indicated in the Gallican liturgical documents. Thus the term *collecta* came to refer to the opening prayer offered by the bishop or priest who was presiding at the eucharist. In Western Christendom, the Roman rite dominated liturgical practice for several centuries, and so the term *collecta*, and its English form *collect*, became the familiar term by which the opening prayer is known down to our own time.

In the next chapter I shall give specific attention to the relation of the collect to the structure of the entrance rite of the eucharist. In the Anglican liturgical tradition, the collect has often been discussed in terms of its relation to the readings from the Bible which follow it, as a kind of preliminary statement of a basic theme to be developed through Scripture. This view is supported by examples of collects which are included by Archbishop Thomas Cranmer in the first two versions of the Book of Common Prayer (1549 and 1552), such as his collect for the Sunday prior to Ash Wednesday (Quinquagesima):

BCP 1549:
O Lord which dost teache us, that all our doinges without charitie are nothyng worthe; sende thy holy gost and powre into oure heartes that moste excellent gyfte of charitie, the very bonde of peace and all vertues, without the whiche, whosoever lyveth is counted dead before thee: Graunt this for thy onely sonne Jesus Christes sake.

[29]

BCP 1979:

O Lord, you have taught us that without love whatever we do is worth nothing: Send your Holy Spirit and pour into our hearts your greatest gift, which is love, the true bond of peace and of all virtue, without which whoever lives is accounted dead before you. Grant this for the sake of your only Son Jesus Christ, who lives and reigns with you and the Holy Spirit, one God, now and for ever. *Amen.*

(Seventh Sunday after Epiphany)

Since at Cranmer's time there was no reading from the Old Testament included in the eucharist, this collect was followed immediately by the First Epistle of St. Paul to the Corinthians, chapter 13, which was the direct inspiration of the collect. In such instances, the connection between the collect and the Scripture which followed was quite evident to the hearers. Yet Cranmer did not make this connection in most cases, and was content to translate or adapt material from the great collection of Latin collects. These were characterized by a more general concern for the needs of the Church. In the next chapter, the idea of a connection between collect and Scripture will be considered more fully in reference to the relation of the collect to the other parts of the eucharistic rite. The early introduction of the collect into the eucharist and its typical content do not support the idea of a link between collect and Scripture, which suggests that this link emerged at a later time, when the original purpose of the collect had become obscured.

Before we consider the role of the collect within the liturgical action, it might be helpful to distinguish its specific form and content as a pattern of prayer. Just as a sonnet is a specific form of poem, so is the collect a specific form of prayer. Although every sonnet is a poem, not every poem is a sonnet. In a sonnet, a formal structure is imposed upon language, and that imposed structure must be adhered to if the end result is to be a sonnet. In the hands of a fine poet, however, the structure does not imprison the language. It is, rather, a case in which the restrictions generate a subtle interplay of images and meanings. Such limits stimulate the creative mind.

What is suggested here about the sonnet applies with equal force to the collect. All collects are prayers, but not all prayers are collects. The distinction refers to the imposed structure. The restriction of the term "collect" to a specific structural pattern may appear as hair-splitting, and it is true that the word is sometimes used indiscriminately for brief prayers in a variety of forms. Words change in meaning and reference, and such evolution is a sign of the vitality of a language. But within the vocabulary of liturgical worship which we have inherited, the designation "collect" refers to a splendid body of prayers which have served the Church as a rich language of common prayer. The fixed structure which is the distinguishing characteristic of the collect-form does not inhibit its validity as *true* prayer. Language always acts as a restraint upon, and a shaper of, prayer. Authentic prayer begins at the still point of a deep interior silence which we shape with words because that is a fundamental means of human communication. In that sense, language is always a somewhat artificial restraint upon prayer because it requires the choice of *these* words rather than those, of certain images rather than others which might serve as well to articulate our interior longing. Words and images are the vast palette from which the choices, consciously or unconsciously, are made. It is this stylization of the collect, this imposed restraint, which gives it a theological significance in Christian liturgical prayer as a kind of microcosm of the underlying framework of the entire liturgical action. The collect is an intense and succinct expression of Trinitarian faith in a specific form of public prayer.

In this perspective, the collect is an image of the entire corporate celebration, a key to its whole purpose. The traditional collect plays a particular role in the eucharist as the summary prayer to the first action of the liturgical assembly, that is, to the gathering of the local church for a common act of faith, a common offering of praise and thanksgiving. The idea of prayer offered in common bears directly upon the posture of the people at this point in the liturgy. Prior to the authorization of the new Book of Common Prayer, the general practice of Episcopalians was to kneel when the priest said "Let us pray" immediately before the collect. This was quite probably a reflection of the adage which was frequently used by clergy to give laity a convenient rule of thumb for participation in public worship: "Stand to praise, kneel to pray, sit to listen." The most obvious problem with this phrase is that it seems to indicate that praise is not a form of prayer, or that what is specifically *prayer* requires a posture associated in the early tradition with private or penitential prayer.

To make this criticism is not meant to suggest that simple pastoral guidelines are not useful; they serve an important purpose in permitting a congregation to get beyond the mechanics of a common body language into the more significant purpose of truly common prayer. But without careful attention, such guidelines, in the name of simplicity and convenience, may betray the deeper purposes of the liturgical action. For the first several centuries of the Church's history, standing was maintained as the posture of common prayer. Kneeling was associated with idolatrous religious practices in the pagan world, and thus was condemned by the Council of Nicaea for the period from Easter to Pentecost and for the Sunday assembly.

> Because there are some who kneel on the Lord's day, and *even* in the days of Pentecost: that all things may be uniformly performed in every parish, it seems good to the holy Synod, that prayers be offered to God standing.[5]

The words "in the days of Pentecost" are a reference to the period of fifty days from Easter to Pentecost in which the Church kept the paschal season, the celebration of the Lord's death and resurrection. For that celebration, the bishops at Nicaea wished to maintain the traditional posture of standing. Kneeling was, as we noted, permitted for Christians engaged in private prayer or in acts of penitence. The collect, on the other hand, was seen as a prayer of the whole gathering, said by the bishop or priest as their representative and as a summary of all their private petitions. The "Let us pray" was a summons to silence for the offering of all these personal concerns, and not a summons to kneel.

In spite of the fact that a standing posture has re-emerged in many parishes for everything that takes place prior to the first reading from Scripture, the collect is often experienced as a kind of liturgical punctuation, as a conclusion to the opening section of the liturgy and as little more than a cue for being seated. We now need a recovery of what the standing posture indicates, namely, that the collect is an important focus of the *common* prayer of all who have gathered. When the people are then seated, they are conscious of themselves *as* a people gathered to listen to the proclamation of the word of God through Scripture and preaching as a community of faith and not as detached individuals.

The people should not find themselves exhausted at this point by a needlessly long entrance rite. Choices as to what elements should or should not be included, whether sung or spoken, must be made with serious attention to the nature of the occasion, the size of the gathering, and the proportions of the building. Too often the shape of the opening rite is determined as a law unto itself, apparently indifferent to these factors, with the result that a kind of liturgical exhaustion is generated at the very beginning of the rite.[6] The arrival at the first reading of Scripture should find the people in an active anticipation of hearing God's word. Being seated is not a posture of passivity, but rather a posture of attention, and it can be that if the first minutes of the liturgy are appropriate to the character of the assembly that day. The effective proclamation of Scripture and the sermon are the first expression of the nourishment which God offers us in the eucharist, later to be complemented by our sacramental nourishment in the eucharistic gifts.

To enable a liturgy to be celebrated in such a corporate spirit will require the emergence of new models of liturgical preparation for which planners, both clergy and laity, will need a high level of sensitivity to the impact of the liturgical experience upon those who gather for worship. There has not been notable evidence of such sensitivity in the development of our inherited models. In these, the dominant role of the clergy both in regard to planning and in the celebration itself has tended to create among the laity in the pews an attitude of passive participation. The recovery of a truly corporate liturgical understanding requires the shaping of models in which there is a truly corporate experience, an experience in which all the people assembled enter into the celebration with a firm sense of themselves as a community of faith participating in a common act of praise.

The development of such a corporate liturgical sense seems to require the rediscovery of the underlying meaning of the liturgical rites. One of the most fruitful ways for such a rediscovery to take place, if I may judge from my own experience in lay education, is to bring people into an engagement with the liturgical texts which we pray week after week. There is an ancient and often-repeated adage which sums up the issue: *lex orandi, lex credendi*, "the law of prayer establishes the law of faith." If we want to know what the Church believes, the saying suggests, then we must look at what the Church prays.

[35]

But to act on this principle is, in fact, to call for a revolution in the way in which liturgical rites are usually engaged by a body of worshippers. The fundamental problem is, as we noted earlier, that liturgical rites have been experienced predominantly as a clerical routine, a kind of liturgical drill. When the laity had a response or some pattern of words to say, this often meant little more than parroting back some words either memorized or printed on the page.

This points to a kind of schizoid attitude with which most Christians have been conditioned to participate in the liturgy. The words of a rite are not seen as having something to do with reality. Rather, they are liturgy, encapsulated in their own world of meaning and thus negligible in regard to potential meaning in the real world. Thus, officiants at Morning Prayer have begun the office with the words, "The Lord is in his holy temple; let all the earth keep silence before him"; then, without even a pause for breath, much less a genuine silence, have continued, "O Lord, open thou our lips." Amusing examples, however, must not permit us to overlook the seriousness of this issue. People have some-how been permitted to ignore the obvious meaning of the words which the rite gives them to say, and we are thus capable again and again of saying the words of the Confession in the liturgy without serious self-examination or a sense of contrition.

I first became aware of this split between liturgy and reality during the years immediately following my ordina-tion. I was working in Latin America, and I inherited a pastoral situation in the missions which I served in which large numbers of people came to me for the baptism of their godchildren. At first I naively went along with the routine, but I soon realized that the promises which the godparents made were not backed by any intention to fulfill them. Nor was this a case of blatant hypocrisy. They had never been led to understand that the promises had any relation to duties which they might have to undertake after the rite was over. The promises were simply words in a book which they were obliged to say if the baby was to be baptized.

Such an extreme example is not as rare as some might think, nor is it limited to the rural environment in which I was living. In great cities this split between liturgy and reality may take a more sophisticated form, but the split is nevertheless present in the accepted attitudes of the participants. This is what I mean when I suggest that we must rediscover what the texts say, and what they ask of us in the realm of faith and action; otherwise the rule of prayer and the rule of faith will remain in conflict. This is why a major dimension of both parochial and seminary education must be an active engagement with what the texts we pray actually say. The split is by no means a problem restricted to the laity. One of the reasons that the isolation of liturgy from reality is so entrenched is that until recently seminary education, even in subjects directly related to liturgical theology and pastoral practice, did not refer to liturgical texts as a basis for theological reflection. One could read treatises on the doctrine of the Holy Spirit, for example, without reference to the liturgical texts which are, *lex orandi*, the primary proclamation of that faith, *lex credendi*.[7]

The focus of this discussion of the prayer book collects offers us a kind of microcosm of this problem and, at the same time, an avenue for renewal. A conscious attention to the nature of the Church's liturgical actions reveals the collect as more than a mere cue that the entrance rite is over and that the people may be seated. If we can reclaim both their content and function, the collects offer an experience of the Church's common prayer, the prayer of the gathered community, and through that experience a participation in the faith which unites us.

The collect is a form of *public* prayer. Among Anglicans, this great treasury of prayer has often served as a resource for private prayer and meditation, as a natural overflow from the prayer of the congregation into the private prayer of the individuals who form that assembly. Such a link between corporate prayer and private prayer is to be encouraged. The great forms of liturgical prayer have been polished through generations of use by the faithful; they are the prayer vocabulary of countless thousands of believers. Yet their source is in the common prayer of the community as a whole. I find them expressive of my needs and concerns because they are the Church's prayer and I am a member of the Church. This suggests the important role of the collect in the unfolding of the liturgical action: it draws all the individual concerns of the members of the assembly into an inclusive form which takes up all these individual petitions into the unity of the Church's common prayer. The fact that the collect is spoken by a bishop or priest who is presiding at a particular liturgy in no way diminishes the corporate significance of the prayer. Rather, it is a potent reminder that the prayer of the ordained leader of the assembly is linked to the role of the ordained person to pray *in the name of the Church*. The "Amen" of the people is its corporate ratification: the collect is the summary of *their* prayer.

During the Sundays of the year, the appointed collects lift up in prayer an astounding array of the concerns of the whole Christian community. If we simply consider the series of collects for the season after Pentecost, Propers 1-6, the corporate character of these petitions is evident, as, for example,

> . . . as you have called us to your service, make us worthy of our calling . . . .

> . . . keep us, we pray, from all things that may hurt us, that we, being ready both in mind and body, may accomplish with free hearts those things which belong to your purpose . . . .

> Grant . . . that your Church may joyfully serve you in confidence and serenity . . . .

> Put away from us, we entreat you, all hurtful things, and give us those things which are profitable for us . . . .

> Grant that by your inspiration we may think those things that are right, and by your merciful guiding may do them . . . .

> Keep, O Lord, your household the Church in your steadfast faith and love, that through your grace we may proclaim your truth with bold-

ness, and minister your justice with compassion
. . . .

These phrases from the collects are typical expressions of
a corporate sense which permeates all these prayers, filled
with the consciousness that the Church has gathered to
pray. These prayers are in their most fundamental
character the common prayers of an assembled body.
They signal to us at the outset that this is not the
coincidence of individual prayers, but the offering of
prayer which pertains to the life of the whole body. Yet
given the powerful influence of privatized attitudes
toward religion which dominate in contemporary society,
the only way to recover the corporate sense of these
prayers in liturgical worship is not merely to hear them
recited, but consciously to engage the theology which
they express. In this way, as a normal dimension of
liturgical formation, the mutual accountability between
what we pray and what we believe, the shaping of the *lex
credendi* by the *lex orandi*, will be fostered.

The Gospel reading holds a primacy in the tradition
as the basis for preaching in the liturgy. The sermon is
not a disjunct element inserted into the rite, a "legitimate
interruption of the liturgy" as one eighteenth-centruy
manual describes it. The sermon is integral to the whole
and thus flows out of the appointed readings; its role is,
in a real sense, to be an extension of the Scripture into
the particular realities of the life of the gathered
community. One hears, on occasion, of sermons being
preached "on the collect," and if this means that the
sermon does not find its generative energy in the
Scripture of the day, then such preaching is to be

discouraged. But given the corporate images which we have seen as characteristic of the collects, their use as a counterpoint, as a complementary theme to the Scripture, will often enrich the resources for liturgical preaching. The task is not one of finding direct links between the collect and one or another of the readings. As we observed earlier, only rarely can such connections be found because the great body of collects were not conceived in that role. Yet often we find a complementarity between the collect and one or more of the readings which will offer a further integration of the sermon into the wider liturgical framework.

The collect for Proper 25, for example, asks God to "increase in us the gifts of faith, hope, and charity; and, that we may obtain what you promise, make us love what you command." When we look at the readings appointed for Cycle A, we find that the Gospel reading (Matthew 22:34-46) is the summary of the law in which Jesus commands us to love God and our neighbor. In Cycle B, the Gospel (Mark 10:46-52) is the encounter between Jesus and Bartimaeus in which the last words of Jesus are, "Go your way; your faith has made you well." Finally, in Cycle C, we find the parable of the Pharisee and the tax collector, in which the penitence of the tax collector is a powerful expression of hope in God. Thus, in all three instances, the collect is found to offer a complementary resource for the development of the sermon.

The appointed readings serve as a kind of focus through which the Church gazes upon the mystery of redemption on a specific Sunday. That mystery is the gift of God's grace revealed in Jesus Christ, but it is like a single diamond with many facets. We approach the one mystery by many different avenues. The diversity of images which we find in the collects of the prayer book does much the same thing. They are, as we have seen, corporate in their basic perspective. They are prayers of the Church gathered. Yet they manifest this ecclesial character through a wide diversity of images, all of which are reflective of our common life in Christ.

Once we begin to reflect on the nature of the liturgical act as a single whole, we see that throughout the entire liturgical action the Church enters again into the reality of God's presence in Christ, participating in the one mystery by attending intensely to some particular aspect of its realization in salvation history. In general terms, the collects for the Sundays of the year ask for God's protection, guidance, grace for service, and the whole range of fundamental needs for which the Church looks to God to provide all its members. The collect appointed for Proper 11 offers a characteristic expression of our dependence upon God to provide for our needs:

> Almighty God, the fountain of all wisdom, you know our necessities before we ask and our ignorance in asking: Have compassion on our weakness, and mercifully give us those things which for our unworthiness we dare not, and for our blindness we cannot ask . . . .

The collects appointed for major feasts and for saints' days quite naturally draw upon the primary image of the feast or of a characteristic particularly associated with the saint who is being commemorated. Yet even with such a narrowing of focus, these collects also express the corporate spirit of the Church's common prayer. The collect for the feast of St. John, for example, picks up the baptismal image of illumination as the primary image of a prayer for the Church:

> Shed upon your Church, O Lord, the bright-
> ness of your light, that we, being illumined
> by the teaching of your apostle and
> evangelist John, may so walk in the light of
> your truth, that at length we may attain to
> the fullness of eternal life . . . .

Once gain, even within the narrowed focus of the particular commemoration of a saint, the prayer is a petition for the whole Church. On such special days, the collect serves to alert the congregation to a particular facet of the liturgical year which the eucharistic rite as a whole will commemorate, but always to the end that the meaning of the feast or the virtue of the saint may be manifested in the Church today.

The wide range of ecclesial concerns which come together within a liturgical rite is imaged in a simple prayer-form which has been hallowed by many centuries of use in the corporate prayer of Western Christians.[8] Although variations within the form may be found, the traditional structure of the collect involves an opening address to God the Father, followed by a clause which describes a quality of God related to the petition which follows, such as God's forgiveness of sins. The petition is the heart of the collect; it is the substance of the prayer for which the formal structure is the setting, and it articulates a concern which touches the lives of the whole community of faith. The petition is what the assembly is asking for itself and, by extension, for the Church as a whole.

The petition is followed by a reference to the result which is hoped for if the petition is granted, and the collect concludes with a Trinitarian doxology which emphasizes the mediating work of Jesus Christ. This full classical pattern is often found in a modified form as one surveys the extensive range of examples in both the Latin and Anglican sources. The following collect for Ash Wednesday offers us an example of the structure in its complete form:

(a) Almighty and everlasting God,

(b) you hate nothing you have made and forgive the sins of all who are penitent:

(c) Create and make in us new and contrite hearts,

(d) that we, worthily lamenting our sins and acknowledging our wretchedness, may obtain of you, the God of all mercy, perfect remission and forgiveness;

(e) through Jesus Christ our Lord, who lives and reigns with you and the Holy Spirit, one God, for ever and ever. *Amen.*

The collects appointed for the Sundays of Lent offer an interesting basis for comparison since they deal with similar or related themes within the same formal structure, yet with a rich diversity of expression. God as the source of contrition and forgiveness of sins, for example, is found in four of the six Sunday collects of Lent, but without duplication of phraseology:

> Come quickly to help us who are assaulted by many temptations; and, as you know the weaknesses of each of us, let each one find you mighty to save . . . . (Lent I)

> Be gracious to all who have gone astray from your ways, and bring them again with penitent hearts and steadfast faith to embrace and hold fast the unchangeable truth of your Word . . . . (Lent II)

> Keep us both outwardly in our bodies and inwardly in our souls, that we may be defended from all adversities which may happen to the body, and from all evil thoughts which may assault and hurt the soul . . . . (Lent III)

> Almighty God, you alone can bring into order the unruly wills and affections of sinners: Grant your people grace to love what you command and desire what you promise . . . . (Lent V)

These examples demonstrate the extraordinary variety which the collect-form can encompass even in the articulation of a single dimension of petitionary prayer.

When we expand our perspective to the whole repertory of collects for the Sundays of the year and other major celebrations, we come face to face with an astounding range of images drawn from both Scripture and the liturgical tradition. The first collect for Easter Day, for example, through a marvelous choice of words and images, conveys the identification of believers with the death and resurrection of Jesus. Whereas this is a clear reference to the meaning of baptism, integral to the Church's celebration of the Easter season, the collect is able at the same time to incorporate an image of the daily dying and living to which Christians are called:

(a) O God,

(b) who for our redemption gave your only-
begotten Son to the death of the cross,
and by his glorious resurrection delivered
us from the power of our enemy:

(c) Grant us so to die daily to sin,

(d) that we may evermore live with him in the
joy of his resurrection;

(e) through Jesus Christ your Son our Lord, who
lives and reigns with you and the Holy Spirit,
one God, now and for ever. *Amen.*

We see here a good example of why the liturgical texts need to be engaged directly in programs of adult education, whether this be in the catechumenate prior to Christian Initiation or in ongoing programs of formation. Without such engagement, the texts remain a merely surface dimension of the weekly liturgical experience. Where such formation is normative, the text of this Easter collect, in spite of the fact that the word "baptism" is not mentioned, is filled with our baptismal identification with the death and resurrection of Jesus.

The connection between baptism and the death and resurrection of Jesus is articulated even more directly in a collect appointed for use at a eucharist celebrated "For all Baptized Christians":

(a/c) Grant, Lord God, to all who have been
       baptized into the death and resurrection
       of your Son Jesus Christ,

(d) that, as we have put away the old life of
     sin, so we may be renewed in the spirit of
     our minds, and live in righteousness and
     true holiness;

(e) through Jesus Christ our Lord, who lives
     and reigns with you, in the unity of the
     Holy Spirit, one God, now and for ever.
     Amen.

Here, God is the source of the grace of baptism. The petition (d) carries an echo of St. Paul's discussion of the new being in the Epistle to the Ephesians (4:22-23), and thus reverberates with images of the Church as the one body, created by the Spirit, and entered into through the one baptism.

It should be immediately evident, even from these few examples, that the collects are not only beautiful forms of prayer, but also prayers which are rich in theological substance. The conscious engagement of these texts becomes an opportunity for the "rule of prayer" and the "rule of faith" to be seen in dynamic interaction. Their Trinitarian closure is consistent with the Trinitarian character of the Great Thanksgiving in the eucharist, thus proclaiming the mediatorial role of Christ and the enlivening work of the Holy Spirit. One begins to perceive the underlying unity of purpose which unites the entire liturgical action.

Joseph Jungmann, in his major study of the Roman rite, speaks of the primacy of the element of petition in the collects.[9] Whereas the Eucharistic Prayer is essentially a prayer of praise and thanksgiving, the focus in the collect is a petition for the Church. In some examples, the form is what Jungmann calls the *simple type*, which is the most direct form of petition, as in, "Father, give us bread," or a joining of address and petition. The second type Jungmann calls the *amplified type* in which the address to God is extended through an added phrase of praise or a description of God's characteristic qualities, such as mercy or love. For example, see this collect for the Sunday of the Passion,

> Almighty and everliving God, in your
> tender love for the human race you sent
> your Son our Savior Jesus Christ to take

upon him our nature, and to suffer death
upon the cross, giving us the example of his
great humility: Mercifully grant that we
may walk in the way of his suffering, and
also share in his resurrection; through Jesus
Christ our Lord, who lives and reigns with
you and the Holy Spirit, one God, for ever
and ever. *Amen,*

or the collect for Proper 21,

O God, you declare your almightly power
chiefly in showing mercy and pity: Grant
us the fullness of your grace, that we, run-
ning to obtain your promises, may become
partakers of your heavenly treasure; through
Jesus Christ our Lord, who lives and reigns
with you and the Holy Spirit, one God, for
ever and ever. *Amen.*

This *amplified type*, according to Jungmann's categories,
is what we have described earlier as the "full classical
pattern" in which the opening address to God the Father
is followed by a clause which describes a quality of God
in light of which the petition will be offered. This full
pattern is especially common in the collects of major feast
days, when the second clause serves to particularize the
focus of the celebration in accord with the theme or
intention of the season or feast.

The collects rest their petitions on the Church's
notions of the nature of God — his love, mercy, forgiveness. The collect for Ash Wednesday quoted earlier

attributes to God some fundamental characteristics which directly affect the lives of Christians. The attributive phrase says, "You hate nothing you have made and forgive the sins of all who are penitent." In this phrase we find implied the doctrine of creation, that God is the "maker of heaven and earth, of all that is, seen and unseen," and that God loves all that exists, including the sinners who resist this creative love. Without this phrase, the text would remain a penitential prayer, but with it we have an image which proclaims the nature of God and at the same time suggests the penitential season of Lent upon which the Church is entering that day. This phrase, in turn, becomes a foundation for the petition for forgiveness which follows. The collect thus serves a structural purpose in drawing the entrance rite to a close and uniting the assembly in a common petition, but it also lifts up the basic image of the new liturgical season.

The same purpose is accomplished in the collect for Easter Day through the attributive phrase,

> who for our redemption gave your only-
> begotten Son to the death of the cross, and
> by his glorious resurrection delivered us
> from the power of our enemy . . . .

Again, we find in this phrase a theology of redemption centered in what is commonly called the paschal mystery, the saving work of God which is held before the world in the death and resurrection of Jesus. The collects are poetic articulations of prayer and at the same time proclamations of Christian faith.

* * * *

Earlier in this chapter I mentioned that in the liturgical pattern of medieval Gaul the *collectio* served to sum up the prayers of the congregation. Thus, in addition to its structural role as a conclusion to the opening rites, the *collectio* refers us to the actual praying of the people. The salutation "The Lord be with you," which precedes the collect, is so often experienced merely as a verbal exchange between the leader and the people that its obvious intention is seldom recognized. The familiar greeting and its response should serve as a kind of liturgical flag, a calling to attention for what is to follow. At this point in the rite, the next phrase serves as a summons to prayer, as the words "Let us pray" clearly show.[10] Yet practically speaking that summons is usually violated by the immediate recitation of the collect, as though the presidential prayer were the only conceivable fulfillment of this summons to prayer. The sense of the collect as a *collecting* of the private prayers of the people is thereby lost. It fulfills its role as an end to the entrance rite, but its relation to the prayer of the assembly is radically obscured. In other words, "Let us pray" is meant to be an invitation to every member of the assembly to offer their own concerns to God in silent prayer. Where a sense of this silent petition has been nurtured, the collect then stands out clearly as the summary prayer of the congregation in which all the individual concerns have been brought into the context of the Church's common prayer.

If the collect is to be experienced as a unifying summary of the people's silent prayer, liturgical formation

[51]

must at some point articulate that purpose in our programs of Christian education. If from childhood a period of prayer had been the ongoing experience of Christians at this point in the liturgy, that experience would itself have shaped an understanding of the silence. The far more common experience, however, is a relentless sequence of words left to the clergy. In this way, at the level of formative experience, the laity have understood their role as essentially passive. The only way that attitude can be corrected is with both the experience of more authentic liturgical models and the appropriate elucidation of those models in our programs of education. Once such models are experienced, the wonderful reciprocity of roles within the liturgical action reveals that the rites are nothing less than an enactment of the Church's being as a community sharing a common life of faith. Diversity and complementarity of gifts within the community. A liturgy which is dominated by a single celebrant images a Church in which ordination is the determining factor of status, but the New Testament gives no support to such a clericalized model. It is baptism which determines Christian status, and on that basis, truly corporate liturgical models are an imperative.

The idea that "Let us pray" is a summons to the assembly for silent prayer is not a romantic fantasy. That is what the words *say*. Unfortunately we have inherited an attitude in which the words of the liturgy are perceived not in their obvious sense, but as formulas to be recited. Our sense of the integrity of liturgical actions cannot possibly be fostered from such abuse of the common sense of language. Liturgical rites are not merely formulas: they are rooted in what the people of God are gathered *to do.*

The intention that the people actually pray is made clear if we look at an ancient pattern of prayer which eventually came to be used only once a year, what we know as the Solemn Collects of Good Friday. This example sheds some light on the role of the collect in the liturgy, since the loss of the regular use of the Solemn Collects was part of a pattern of structural changes in the liturgy to which the emergence of the collect is related. There is documentation from the sixth century which indicates an expansion of the invitation to prayer by a phrase stating the intention for which the people were to pray. The deacon then said, "Let us bend the knee," and the people knelt for a time of silent prayer. After the people were summoned to stand, the celebrant then recited a collect to bring the prayer for that intention to a conclusion. This pattern continued for a whole series of intentions and collects.

In the rites for Holy Week in the Book of Common Prayer, the Solemn Collects have been introduced to the Anglican liturgical tradition for the first time through official authorization. Given the diversity of practice which characterizes Anglican liturgical norms, the rite wisely does not set a fixed pattern of kneeling or standing, as is characteristic of the book as a whole, and is content simply to indicate by rubric that *"The people may be directed to stand or kneel."* Far more important is the fact that the integrity of the form has been maintained through the rubrical indication that silence is to be observed after each set of intentions has been said and before the summary collect. Thus, at least on Good

Friday, the authentic character of the collect as a conclusion to the silent prayer of the people has been recovered.

The Solemn Collects offer us an important example from the Church's ancient liturgical tradition of the relation of the collect-form to the individual prayers of the members of the assembly. The version in the Book of Common Prayer has the deacon or some other person appointed invite the people to pray for a list of intentions. In this particular form, the intentions pertain to the general concerns of the Church, its unity, the clergy, all Christians and those about to be baptized. In the second bidding, the horizon of prayer extends to all the nations of the earth, and those who are in positions of authority. The third bidding is concerned with all who suffer; the fourth, with those "who have not received the Gospel of Christ," including all who are alienated from or at enmity with the Church. Finally, the people are invited to pray for themselves and for all the departed, that all of us "may be accounted worthy to enter into the fullness of the joy of our Lord, and receive the crown of life in the day of resurrection." After another period of silence for the prayers of the people, the final collect of the series is a long prayer for the whole Church. This prayer enlarges the traditional form with a series of petitions, which build upon images of God's saving work in the renewal of all things.

> O God of unchangeable power and eternal
> light: Look favorably on your whole
> Church, that wonderful and sacred mystery;
> by the effectual working of your provi-

dence, carry out in tranquillity the plan of salvation; let the whole world see and know that things which were cast down are being raised up, and things which had grown old are being made new, and that all things are being brought to their perfection by him through whom all things were made, your Son Jesus Christ our Lord; who lives and reigns with you, in the unity of the Holy Spirit, one God, for ever and ever. *Amen.*

This same prayer reappears in the Easter Vigil after the last Old Testament reading, thus making a palpable link between the two rites and serving as a clear indication that for Christians the great sign of God's bringing new life out of old, and resurrection out of death, is seen in the dying and rising of Jesus.

The silence required by the rubrics for the Solemn Collects and prior to the collects of the Vigil readings is a significant recovery, at least potentially, of the role of corporate silence in the context of liturgical prayer. The Book of Common Prayer of 1979 has also restored the practice of silence to its legitimate role at other places in the rites, notably in the various forms of the Prayers of the People and also "at many points where a period of recollection or reflection is appropriate."[11] Unfortunately, a silence is not called for by rubric immediately prior to the collect in the rites for either the eucharist or the daily offices. One may suggest, however, that the invitation "Let us pray " implies such a period, during which the members of the assembly may offer prayer for personal concerns in silence. Through an appropriate liturgical catechesis, such a silence would offer a major opportunity for the formation of a bridge between the daily private prayer of individual Christians and their integration into the corporate framework of the Church's prayer.

It follows from our discussion of the collect as a summary prayer, that only one collect is needed to accomplish its role as a conclusion. The 1979 Book of Common Prayer implies that one collect should be normative. The rubrics for the collect in the eucharist do not suggest the addition of extra collects, and even in Morning and Evening Prayer, the rubric suggests one collect as the first option at the conclusion of the office. Old patterns persist, however, and the use of several collects in the office in many places maintains the idea that liturgical prayer is something which the celebrant or officiant does on behalf of the assembly, rather than what the whole gathering is involved in doing. The 1928 BCP continued the Prayer Book tradition of reciting multiple collects even in the eucharist, in certain seasons, a tradition which grew out of the loss in the middle ages of the structural role of the collect as a summary prayer. The collect for Advent I and the collect for Ash Wednesday were authorized for daily recitation during the seasons which they initiated, thus emphasizing their role in establishing the character of a particular season of the Church Year. Such repetitions have been done away with in the 1979 BCP, perhaps an indication of a recovery of the understanding of the collect which I am proposing in this chapter.

For almost a thousand years, documents indicate that only one collect was used in the Western rites. Even when two feasts happened to fall on the same day, only one collect was used.[12] There eventually developed the custom of combining two distinct petitions or themes into one collect, and by the ninth century we have examples of the addition of a second collect. Along with the multiplication of collects, we also find the expansion of the form into long verbal patterns which became characteristic of the northern European rites. Under the influence of medieval numerological symbolism, there eventually emerged a regulation that never more than seven collects should be used, and always an uneven number — seven, five, three or one. It seems that no more than seven might be used so as not to exceed the petitions of the Lord's Prayer, and an uneven number is favored as a symbol of indivisibility and unity. It is obvious that factors were then shaping the use of the collect that had nothing to do with the purposes for which it had been first introduced. Three collects were especially favored because, of course, this symbolized the Holy Trinity!

This multiplication of the number of collects points us to the significant structural shift which emerged when the Prayers of the People were lost from the eucharistic rite. With the loss of the primitive intercession, there developed an inevitable pressure for the creation of a focus for the special concerns and intentions of the Church. An increase in the number of collects offered a solution, perhaps at an unconscious level, to that need. The multiplication of collects which emerges in the medieval documents is a potent sign of the loss of the intercessory role of the laity as the priest came more and more to control the liturgical action. The evolution of this structural shift changed the Church's perception of the collect within the liturgical rites and obscured its communal character. It is to this aspect of liturgical history that we now turn.

> Almighty and everlasting God, by whose Spirit the whole body of your faithful people is governed and sanctified: Receive our supplications and prayers, which we offer before you for all members of your holy Church, that in their vocation and ministry they may truly and devoutly serve you; through our Lord and Savior Jesus Christ, who lives and reigns with you, in the unity of the Holy Spirit, one God, now and for ever. *Amen.*

(Collect for all Christians in their vocation)

Chapter Three

Structuring the Community's Prayer

In the previous chapter, I·tried to suggest that public worship is a very simple thing in terms of its essentials. A group of people who share a common faith gather together and *do something*. What they do is not at all arbitrary in regard to those essentials because what they do in such an assembly is a direct image of what they understand themselves to be, the people of God.

Once gathered, the first essential is the telling of some aspect of their common story. This is accomplished through public reading, what is usually known as the Liturgy of the Word, or the proclamation of the Word of God. The placing of the reading of Scripture toward the beginning of all liturgical rites is not simply a convenient way to make sure that people become acquainted with the Bible. They are a people called and formed by the Word of God, and the proclaiming of that Word at each liturgical assembly places the pieces of the life of faith in their proper relation: the initiative for the forming of the Church as a community of faith lies with God. It is God who calls us; we respond to that call. The ordered reading of Scripture, especially in the Sunday assembly week after week, serves as nourishment to our common memory of how God has acted in human history to save all people and to call them into membership in God's family, the Church.

In this regular proclamation from the books of the Bible, there is created a context in which the life experience of each individual may be more deeply illuminated by the Church's common story. In the story of the salvation of the world, each one of us comes to see our own personal story of salvation, how God has acted and continues to act not only in history in general but also in *my* history. The biblical story comes to be seen as a mirror which holds together in focus all the individual stories of men and women throughout history.

This interplay between corporate and individual aspects of salvation history forms an obvious parallel to the interplay between corporate and individual aspects of prayer which we discussed in the previous chapter. The liturgical assembly is the place where this interplay is supposed to happen, the occasion at which I as an individual, with my own particular identity and range of experience, join with my sisters and brothers in Christ to celebrate the presence and grace of God in this wonderful intersection of the universal and the particular.

In this perspective, the role of the sermon emerges with a new vitality. The lectionary gives the Church an ordered pattern for the reading of Scripture so that, under normal circumstances, all the various assemblies in parishes and missions all over the nation hear the same readings and thus share in the proclamation of the same facets of our common story. The sermon then brings in the dimension of particularity. For the preacher, who is usually a person with pastoral oversight in the local community, takes this common proclamation of the Word of God as the basis for a sermon which seeks to discern the way the Scripture readings touch the life of this particular community, in this place and at this time. Differences between a sermon preached in one community and that preached in another do not lie in the fundamentals of the gospel proclamation, but rather in the ways in which these fundamentals of faith are used to penetrate and illuminate anew the life of a particular community of faith.

After the sermon, the local community, renewed in its sense of its identity as the people of God, expresses its stewardship toward the needs of the world. The Prayers of the People are a natural response to the proclamation of the Word of God that commissions us as instruments of the will of God — even, in a sense, as co-redeemers — as we seek to realize God's purposes in the world around us.

The last of the essential dimensions of public worship is the sacramental act, which embodies and proclaims our identity as the people of God. The Word proclaimed finds its deepest complementarity in the Word signified, for, as St. Augustine taught, the sacrament is "the Word made visible." The significance of the eucharist in the life of the Church is seen in this interplay of the universal and the particular mentioned above. It is the common act of Christians throughout history and all over the world, and is based upon a human action of a dazzling simplicity, a shared meal of thanksgiving to God. To acknowledge this common human action at the heart of the eucharist is to affirm again the essentially corporate nature of Christian prayer. In the classical Anglicanism of the seventeenth century, the eucharist was seen as the place at which the members of the Church experience, Sunday after Sunday, their shared baptismal identity. The liturgical celebration of Christian faith always points to the common life of the Body of Christ. The sharing of the eucharistic gifts gives believers direct experience of their unity in Christ, "one bread, one body."

Once this sign of unity has been shared, there remains only for the believers to depart, to be sent forth to put into action in daily life the stewardship of the creation that is given to us as the people of God. The concerns which have been lifted up in prayer now become the tasks of a common ministry in the world, each one of us acting in terms of the diversity of gifts which the Holy Spirit gives to the members of the body. This is the extensive dimension of the eucharist, as the members of the Church, renewed in their self-awareness as the Body of Christ go forth to be Christ in the world.

Beneath all these descriptive words, there is a liturgical structure of remarkable simplicity: gathering, telling the story, praying for the world, sharing in a meal of thanksgiving. To a great extent, the early pattern of the eucharist was restricted very much to these elements.

Gradually, however, under the influence of changing cultural and social circumstances, a wide range of secondary elements began to cluster around the basic structure. Many of these developments corresponded in appropriate ways to diverse and changing pastoral situations but often such accretions, although appropriate in a given context, came to be virtually equated with the essentials which we considered above. Elements of quite secondary significance came to be as fixed a part of the liturgical tradition as primary elements, and the underlying simplicity of the rite came gradually to be obscured and its purpose as an act of common prayer to be undermined.

In this chapter we shall be looking at this tendency in terms of the structural evolution of the eucharistic rite, giving special attention to the ways in which this evolution came gradually to inhibit the Church's understanding of the liturgy as the community gathered to pray. Examining the way that the collect functions in the eucharistic rite offers us a convenient focus for an overview of this evolution.

The development of the various parts of the eucharistic rite has been the object of a variety of interpretations among liturgical historians, and this diversity applies at least as much to the collect as to any other aspect of the rite. Some writers have emphasized the relation of the collect of the entrance rite, a view which we explored in the previous chapter. This view is based upon the possible link between *collectio* and *collecta*, and suggests that the origin of this prayer-form is found in the custom which was popular in Rome of having the people gather out of doors at a place which was known as a "station."

There a prayer was offered, and then the clergy and people walked in procession to an appointed church where the liturgy was celebrated. This out-of-doors assembly, as noted in the previous chapter, was known as a *collecta*.

Another view is that the collect is a conclusion to the *Kyrie*, which, as we shall see in this chapter, is a vestige of an entrance litany. Current research, however, suggests that the collect appeared in the eucharist a half-century prior to the introduction of the litany. This does not, of course, exclude the possibility of the litany-collect relation, but it does suggest that the origin of the collect as a prayer-form must be looked for elsewhere. In Jungmann's analysis of the question, it is sometimes difficult to discern when he is giving a rationale for the fully developed entrance rite in the Missal of Pius V (1570) and when he is pointing to an earlier stratum of liturgical orgins.[1] In order to gain some clarity on this issue, we must examine the wider picture of the development of the structure of the eucharist.

In our earliest documents on the eucharistic rite, there is no evidence of the inclusion of an opening prayer. The *First Apology* of Justin Martyr, which dates from the middle of the second century, describes the pattern of the eucharistic celebration at the Sunday assembly. The relevant text reads as follows:

> On the day named after the sun, all who
> live in city or countryside assemble, and the
> memoirs of the apostles or the writings of
> the prophets are read for as long as time
> allows. When the lector has finished, the

president addresses us, admonishing us and exhorting us to imitate the splendid things we have heard. When we all stand and pray, and, as we said earlier, when we have finished praying, bread, wine, and water are brought up. The president offers prayers of thanksgiving, according to his ability, and the people give their assent with an 'Amen!' Next, the gifts over which the thanksgiving has been spoken are distributed, and each one shares in them, while they are also sent via the deacons to the absent brethren.[2]

Since Justin's treatise was written for a non-Christian audience, as an explanation of what Christians believe and do, it uses the common language of contemporary Roman society. For example, in Justin's reference to the astrological designation of the first day of the week he uses the phrase, "the day named after the sun" rather than the Christian designation, "the day of the Lord." Considering Justin's audience, it is not surprising that he does not give detailed information about the liturgy. What he describes, however, is a pattern which has continued to provide the essential elements of a eucharistic celebration, in spite of various ritual elaborations, in all the centuries since Justin's time: Scripture, homily, intercession, eucharistic prayer and communion.

Justin refers explicitly to only two types of prayer: the prayers offered by the assembly (what we call the Prayers of the People), and the prayers of thanksgiving (the Great Thanksgiving). In other words, we find no indication in the *First Apology* that a collect or some form of opening prayer was part of the rite. We easily tend to read backward into the early liturgy practices that developed later and are now taken for granted. Liturgical research has revealed an organic development of the structure of the various liturgical rites, and there is certainly no reason to suspect that there was any type of collect in the second century which Justin has simply failed to mention. The evidence is that the Christian Sunday assembly began directly with the reading of Scripture. There was no introductory rite at all, nor was there need for one, since Christians gathered in a context of intimacy and trust, usually in a private home.

Christians have been accustomed for so many centuries to gathering for worship in buildings especially built for that purpose that it is difficult for us to imagine how different the situation was during the early times of persecution. We also tend to take for granted a whole range of secondary elements. The entrance procession with acolytes, choir, and cross, for example, would have been unimaginable during years when Christian assembly for worship was, in the best of times, only tolerated, and in the worst of times actively opposed. It was only after Christians began to enjoy the privilege of freedom of worship, once Constantine issued his edict of toleration in 313 A.D., that a public ritual of gathering could begin to develop in connection with the eucharist. Such a ritual was an indication that Christians had moved from private places of assembly into the large public buildings that were now made available to the Church. Prior to that important transition, the eucharistic liturgy was characterized by those essential elements spoken of earlier in this chapter. Once gathered, even if that involved only a coming together in an appointed place, the first essential was the reading of Scripture. Thus, if we look to the documents written prior to the early fourth century, we find laid out the groundplan which has remained the essential shape of Christian worship ever since.

The basic description of the Sunday assembly which Justin gives us in about 150 A.D. still holds true some sixty years later, according to a document which has deeply influenced liturgical research in this century. This later work, entitled *Apostolic Tradition*, offers us somewhat more detailed information, but there is nothing in it which contradicts the description given by Justin which I quoted above. In other words, the material which has come down to us from the first three centuries of Christian history is consistent in regard to the fundamental pattern of the Sunday assembly. In *Apostolic Tradition*, as in the *First Apology*, there is no indication of some form of opening prayer or collect, and this lack seems to point to an informality in the first stage of gathering and not to the type of ritualized pattern which developed later.[3]

The dominant language of the Christian community during years prior to its liberation by Constantine was Greek and so, as should be expected, both the *First Apology* and *Apostolic Tradition* were written in Greek. The gradual transition from Greek to Latin as the language of the liturgy began in the middle of the third century, a few decades after *Apostolic Tradition* was written. The transition took approximately a century, and came to completion by about 380 A.D.[4] The shift in language seems to have contributed to a new flowering of

[67]

liturgical creativity. The expansion of the Church after its liberation by Constantine led to an increasing need for the delegation of pastoral authority from the bishop. When faith in Christ no longer involved the risk of persecution, the size of the Christian community expanded rapidly. Whereas during times of persecution, a comparatively small number of Christians might gather secretly with their bishop to celebrate the eucharist on Sunday, the expansion of the Church meant that it was no longer physically possible for all the baptized to gather in one place. Therefore a gradual process began in which the bishop delegated pastoral responsibility to his council of presbyters, who thus came through a natural evolution to take up sacramental oversight which had normally been identified with the bishop.

Liturgical prayer had developed essentially as an oral tradition, not as a set of fixed formulas to be rigidly repeated. There was thus a coinciding between the extension of pastoral/liturgical oversight with the shift to the use of Latin, which had gradually become the dominant language in Roman society. The new liturgical creativity, witnessed to by the abundance of Latin texts which have come down to us, is evidence of the Church's adjustment to a radically altered pastoral situation. Whereas both the *First Apology* and *Apostolic Tradition* presume some ability on the part of the one presiding at the eucharist to proclaim the Church's faith in spontaneous prayer based upon the oral tradition, the extension of pastoral responsibility to meet the needs of increased numbers of Christians inevitably led to a gradual regularization or standardization of the patterns of public prayer. At the same time, it must have become obvious very soon that ordination did not necessarily carry with it a gift for spontaneous public prayer.

In the light of this evolution, it is not surprising that by the end of fourth century, a century that saw significant expansion in the Church, written forms of prayer began to take the place of the spontaneous prayers which had characterized liturgical ministry during preceding centuries. The fourth century also saw the development of the liturgical calendar, especially in regard to the incorporation of commemorations of various saints. Out of this time of liturgical change, there developed a considerable elaboration of liturgical rites during the following century. Pope Celestine I (422-432 A.D.) is credited with the introduction of an entrance chant which used texts from the psalter to accompany the entry of the ministers into large public buildings. This *Introit* led directly to the readings from Scripture with no intervening prayer. So to this point, it would seem, the collect had not yet been introduced.

The dating of the entrance psalm at the time of Pope Celestine I helps us to bring into focus the first appearance of the collect. Only a few years after the death of Celestine, Leo I (440-461 A.D.) was elected to the papacy, and seems likely to have been the person who introduced the collect into the structure of the eucharist. The evidence, however, is somewhat indirect.[5] In approximately 570 A.D., a collection of prayers for the eucharist was compiled which is known as the Verona Sacramentary. These texts were once attributed to Leo, but recent scholarship has indicated that they are the work of several authors, Leo among them. The collection contains a variety of liturgical materials, including a number of collects. The collect for the second Sunday after Christmas, for example, has been familiar to Anglicans through various collections of prayers, but has been included officially in the American Book of Common Prayer beginning only with the 1979 version. Recent scholarship has indicated that this collect is the work of Leo I, found among the materials attributed to him in the Verona Sacramentary. The text of the collect gives us a classical example of its traditional form:

> O God, who wonderfully created, and yet more wonderfully restored, the dignity of human nature: Grant that we may share the divine life of him who humbled himself to share our humanity, your Son Jesus Christ; who lives and reigns with you, in the unity of the Holy Spirit, one God, for ever and ever. *Amen.*

Scholars have determined that this collect was written by Leo, and this conclusion is based on studies of his language in other writings, such as his sermons. These links in literary style are generally accepted as a reliable basis for establishing authorship, at least with a reasonable degree of confidence. If Leo is the author of the collects attributed to him, it would seem to follow that they were composed for use in liturgical celebrations at which he presided. The collect was seen by Leo as a prayer which, along with the Proper Preface used in the same celebration, offered a means by which a specific aspect of the Christian mystery of redemption would be focused and proclaimed before the gathered faithful. In this example, the feast is Christmas, and in the Verona Sacramentary we find this collect appointed for the first eucharist of Christmas Day.[6] Following the structure inherited from his predecessor, Celestine, Leo would thus have inserted the collect as a kind of concluding focus to the entrance psalm which would, at the same time, have sounded the central theme of the feast.

As the Church adjusted to the reality of its freedom and its emergence as a power within society, significant modifications developed in its pattern of public worship. The essentially simple structure that is set forth in the *First Apology* and *Apostolic Tradition* began to be elaborated and even rearranged under the impact of the Church's new public situation. The structural changes which we have ascribed to Celestine and Leo were only part of a much more complex picture.

In our discussion of the Solemn Collects in the previous chapter, we observed how they were related to the silent prayer of the people gathered as a formal summary and conclusion to that common prayer. From a structural perspective, however, the Solemn Collects are also related to the major shifts which were taking place in the eucharistic rite. In our earlier discusison of Justin's *First Apology*, we observed that already in the mid-second century there is clear evidence for the inclusion of an intercession by the assembly after the readings and homily. This intercessory element in Christian worship, what the 1979 Book of Common Prayer calls "the Prayers of the People," is a major expression of continuity between the liturgical pattern of the synagogue and that of the early centuries of the Church. As Christian liturgical rites developed, a distinct contrast emerged between the form of the intercession in East and West.

In an interesting study of intercessory prayer in the liturgy, G. G. Willis has contrasted the Eastern and Western patterns.[7] In the Eastern rites, he notes, the great range of classes of people for whom the congregation is asked to pray is quite remarkable, but this is accomplished with an economy of form. In the Western tradition, the list of concerns is much more succinct and focused, with a logical grouping of concerns which seems to have been characteristic of the Western rite. With its introductory series of intentions, the Western form developed as a somewhat heavily clerical pattern, whereas the Eastern form involved frequent responses from the people. In the West, the fundamental concerns included: the Church and its peace; the bishop and all the ordained, and the whole people of God; rulers; catechumens; those suffering from disease, famine, and imprisonment; and for those who travel. As we observed in the previous chapter, each intention concluded with the phrase, "Let us pray," as an invitation to the people to offer silent prayer. The silence was ended by the celebrant with a collect which summed up the silent prayer of the people. This is, of course, the pattern of intercession now included in the American Book of Common Prayer for Good Friday.

In its original context, however, this form of intercession was not limited to a single occasion in the year. It was, rather, the standard form of intercession in the Western eucharist. As a result, the comprehensiveness of the series of intentions and collects as a truly ecclesial intercession also involved a practical difficulty: it was a form of intercession which took a significant amount of *time* when compared to other elements in the rite. The gradual elaboration of the liturgy from the fourth century, and the growth in the size of the Sunday assemblies, seem to have led to pressure for structural reform. The need emerged for some regulation of the various parts of the rite to arrive at a less wearisome length. The Eastern rites, with their litany form, seemed to offer an appropriate alternative. In this type, the deacon announced an intention in a short phrase, which received an immediate response from the congregation with a phrase such as *Kyrie eleison.* The litany concluded with a final collect by the one presiding, rather than a series of collects. The litany offered a more brief pattern for intercessory prayer, but at the same time removed from the congregation the opportunity for silent prayer through which their individual concerns might be taken into the corporate framework of the Church's public prayer. It is ironic that what at first gave the people a greater verbal participation was at the same time a significant loss in regard to the use of silence in the liturgy as an occasion for common prayer.[8] It could not have been perceived at the time, but these developments were part of a gradual restructuring of the liturgical celebration in ways which would eventually lead to the loss of any essential involvement of the laity in the eucharistic offering. The signs were already beginning to emerge of a mentality in which the liturgical rites would be seen as the exclusive domain of the ordained.

It was toward the end of the fifth century, during the pontificate of Pope Gelasius I (492-496), that the litany type of intercession was introduced into the Roman eucharistic rite. Although modelled upon the Eastern form, the new litany was in Latin, which had been the language of worship at Rome for over a century. It seems likely that at the same time that the litany was introduced, it was also moved to the opening of the entire rite and became an entrance litany. Since, as we have seen, the opening collect had appeared earlier in the century, that prayer and the concluding collect of the litany would have coalesced into the final prayer of the entrance rite. The collect inserted by Leo to conclude the entrance psalm and the usual closing collect of the intercession thus drew together into a single function as the conclusion of the entrance rite.

The natural conservatism of the Roman rite is seen in the consequent fate of the Western pattern of intercession, the series of intentions, silence and collects. Gelasius preserved that pattern on two days of the year, the Wednesday and Friday of Holy Week, on which days the older pattern of beginning directly with the readings was preserved.[9] In the end, this pattern survived only on Good Friday, and has been recovered for the Anglican liturgical tradition in the rite for Good Friday in the American Prayer Book.

The last significant stage in this structural evolution took place a century later during the pontificate of Gregory the Great (590-604). The decision of Constantine in the fourth century to make Constantinople the center of government had created a kind of leadership vacuum at Rome which had significant impact upon the papal office. Although the pope's authority was clearly derived from his office in the Church, it also came to acquire increasing political importance. The papal liturgies became more than important religious events; because of his role in Roman society, liturgical events became occasions of enormous social significance as well. Given this situation, it is not surprising that the problem of inordinate length of liturgical rites continued to affect decisions about liturgical structure. Gregory the Great combined a wide range of abilities which had direct impact upon various dimensions of the Church's life. Among these was Gregory's concern for the revision, simplification and reorganization of the Roman rite. In line with those concerns, as part of Gregory's reform of the liturgy, the litany was shortened, and yet more drastically, on ordinary days which involved no special solemnity, the deacon's petitionary phrases were eliminated, leaving only the congregational response: *Kyrie eleison*, with the complementary phrase *Christe eleison*, which had been added during the course of the preceding century. Within a short time we have documentary evidence that the petitionary phrases were dropped entirely, leaving only the expanded *Kyrie*, which now became a hymn sung by the choir, and the concluding collect.

With this final stage of the process, intercessory prayer by the whole congregation in the context of the liturgy was completely lost. The intercessory needs of the Church had now been taken entirely into the eucharistic prayer, which was by the early seventh century at the latest offered in virtual silence by the celebrant. Thus the intercessions, which had been a fundamental part of the role of the laity in the primitive eucharist, were not only clericalized but even ceased to be heard. This is not to suggest that the people ceased to intercede for their own needs and the needs of others. But such intercession, which had played so fundamental a role as the expression of the prayers of the people in the early centuries of liturgical development, was now effectively excluded from the central act of Christian worship. The collect as a prayer-form retained its place in the liturgical structure, but it lost any explicit connection with the personal concerns of the laity.

The only exception to this may be found in the emergence of what is called the votive mass, from the Latin *votum*, meaning wish or desire. These were celebrations of the eucharist for the special concerns of a small group or even of a single person, a type of specialized intercession.[10] For these votives, the official calendar of the Church could be ignored for the sake of the special concern, which found particular intercessory expression in the collect. There were numerous sets of such votive masses provided for a range of concerns, but by far the most common (and the most abused) was that known as the requiem mass, that is, a eucharist offered for a deceased person. The economic abuses of such masses as a source of income for the Church is too well documented to require further attention here, but what is of special interest to this discussion is the way in which such votive masses served to replace the intercessory opportunity of the laity within the context of the eucharist. In votives, such as a requiem for a departed family member, the mention of the person's name in the collect fulfilled a fundamental need which the structural change had excluded, and thus restored intercession to the people's experience of the eucharist.

Our discussion of the collect thus far has emphasized its relation to the intercessory aspects of the eucharist. Even the loss of the intercession as a structural part of the rite did not totally obscure this dimension of the collect-form, although it diminished its significance in that regard. There is evidence, however, for a different approach to the role of the collect in the Western liturgical tradition. The historical material which we have considered up to this point has related the collect to the early evolution of an entrance rite, and then somewhat later the fusion of that with the role of the collect as a conclusion to the intercessions of the liturgical assembly. In both of these, as we have noted, the collect has been connected with common prayer or corporate intercession, two somewhat distinct purposes being served by the same form of prayer. Given the organic and at the same time conservative character of liturgical evolution, such fusion may be suggested as a typical characteristic of developing ritual patterns.

We may now add to this yet a third contributing factor in the origins of the collect. This third perspective is not intended to contradict the two considered thus far, but rather to furnish evidence of yet another energy underlying the collect-form as its place in the Western rite was established. The third dimension of the collect is found in the occasional evidence of a relation between it and the scriptural readings that followed. The Anglican liturgical scholar Gregory Dix has suggested that the collect emerged as a link to the Scripture, and points to our earliest source for the Egyptian rite, the sacramentary of Serapion (c. 340). There, a prayer is placed prior to the readings and is clearly related to them. The text of this prayer reads in part:

> Send the Holy Spirit into our mind and give
> us grace to learn the divine Scriptures from
> the Holy Spirit, and to interpret cleanly and
> worthily, that all the laity here present may
> be helped . . . .

Dix notes that relations between Alexandria and Rome
were particularly close during the middle of the fifth
century, and suggests that, as is certainly the case with
the importation of other Eastern liturgical practices, these
links facilitated the adoption of this Egyptian practice.
The invariable Eastern form was reshaped under the
influence of the restrained Roman literary style, and soon
became a variable prayer, as is evident from the collects
of the Verona Sacramentary.[11]

G. G. Willis accepts Dix's thesis, and on the basis of
examples in Eastern rites proposes that other theories
about the role of the collect should be put aside; the
collect is related to what *follows*, and not to what comes
before it.[12] But is it necessary to espouse one view to the
exclusion of the others? Any overview of the evolution
of liturgical rites, especially from the fourth century
onward, suggests that many factors, cultural, social and
political, exerted pressure upon the patterns of Christian
worship. It was never merely a question of authoritative
decisions made by the leadership of the Church, even
when that leadership involved such dynamic personalities
as Leo or Gelasius or Gregory. The social character of
liturgical celebrations suggests a more natural evolution in
which even the introduction of new elements does not

involve the annihilation of the old, but rather modification and adaptation. We have observed that gradual process in connection with the intercessory material in the eucharist, and it seems likely that the collect, too, is the fruit of such a gradual fusion of diverse pressures as the eucharistic rite was itself progressively modified. The theory that the collect is related to the readings has, however, been especially favored in Anglican apologetical writings on the liturgy, and we will turn to that question now.

The eucharistic rite in the first Book of Common Prayer (1549) gives no indication of what I have referred to in this book as an "entrance rite." The first rubric pertaining to the rite itself says simply:

> *The Priest standyng humbly afore the middes of the Altar, shall saie the Lordes praier, with this Collect.*

The text for the prayer known as the Collect for Purity follows, and then a rubric indicating the recitation of the psalm verses appointed for the day. These are printed elsewhere in the prayer book together with what are known as the propers of the day, namely, "the introites, collectes, epistles, and gospels, to be used at the celebracion of the Lordes Supper and Holye Communion throughe the yeare." The appointed psalm verses, or introit, are followed by the nine-fold *Kyrie*, the *Gloria in excelsis* (both in English), the salutation, the collect of the day, and then one of two invariable collects appointed as prayer for the king.[13] It is important to note the details of this elaborate pattern, for we find buried within it vestigial elements of the classical entrance rite that I talked about earlier in this study, but in a context which significantly obscures the original sense of these diverse elements. What we have in the above summary is a massive block of verbal material all said by the priest. The rubrics permit the possible alternative that the "clerkes" might sing the *Kyrie* and *Gloria*, but there is no reference to any participatory role on the part of the people.

Where did this material come from? The psalm verses of the introit we recognize as a vestige of the entrance chant authorized by Pope Celestine I to accompany the entrance of the clergy into large buildings of public assembly. The *Kyrie* is a vestige of the intercessory litany that Pope Gelasius introduced as a replacement for the collects which had formed the intercession of the Western eucharist; he seems to have used it as an alternative to the introit psalm of Celestine. The *Gloria in excelsis*, apparently intended in the 1549 Book of Common Prayer for use at every celebration of the eucharist, was first introduced as a hymn at morning prayer, probably in the fourth century, but came into the eucharist very gradually and then only as a distinctive element for major feasts.[14]

The celebrant's salutation to the people, "The Lord be with you," is the ancient greeting which had always summoned the people to silent prayer. Yet in the 1549 Book of Common Prayer there is no indication that such silence was expected, for the rubric indicates that the collect of the day will follow directly. The two forms of prayer for the king are clearly intercessory in character, and are thus examples of the shift of intercessory material into the place of the collect. In addition to this, it should be noted that in the 1549 Eucharistic Prayer, Archbishop Cranmer retained a large block of intercessory material which was later separated as the prayer "for the whole state of Christes Church militant here in earth" in the 1552 Prayer Book. This intercessory material also includes prayer for the monarch, and is a reminder of the shift of such material from the prayers of the people into a clericalized context within the Eucharistic Prayer.

In other words, this opening material from the 1549 rite for the eucharist is a hodgepodge, the throwing together of a grab bag of liturgical materials. Most of these had developed in the context of large assemblies of people in grand public buildings, as material appropriate to the opening ritual of a significant religious and social event — a kind of gathering and entrance rite as the ministers approached the altar. In the 1549 rite, *all* of this material takes place after the priest has arrived at the altar. It is no wonder that one contemporary liturgist has referred to this confused amalgam as "our cluttered vistibule,"[15] for the problem which persists in modern liturgical books is the result of a piling up of liturgical layers with little awareness of the source of various materials, or of the role which they were originally intended to play.

It has been necessary to go into some detail on this background in order to understand how the collect came to be seen, especially in Anglicanism and other Reformed traditions, as a prayer related to the readings. In the pileup of liturgical layers which was described above, we have a situation in which the function of individual liturgical elements becomes radically obscured and in which a new sense of function emerges from a reshaped pattern of liturgical experience. The point here is not that the new sense is incorrect, for within the new context it is quite understandable. It is rather that the new sense becomes the basis for a liturgical apologetic which has lost its rooting in the historical evolution of patterns of worship.

The sequence of elements in the eucharistic rite of 1549 presumes a ritual framework quite different from that in which its various elements had been shaped. This is nowhere more evident than in regard to the collect. In the early middle ages, the collect came as the conclusion to a ritual action, and in this regard it does not really matter whether it was the conclusion to a litany or a prayer after an entrance psalm — in both cases, its functional effect was the same. But in the 1549 pattern, the collect comes at a point when a number of elements have already been said at the altar, so it was, at the level of experience, quite impossible to think of the collect as a conclusion to an entrance rite: the liturgical structure had ceased to function in that way.

In other words, behind the rite which Cranmer prepared lay the formative experience of a said mass, a celebration completely performed by a single priest and entirely focused at the altar. During the generations immediately prior to the Reformation, frequent lay attendance at mass was greatly encouraged. Yet except for people living near a great monastic community or an important cathedral, the experience of the mass would normally have been in its most deprived form, without the musical and ritual dimensions which had been standard in the time, for example, of Gregory the Great.

The Reformers were all concerned to remove abuses and superstition from the Church's worship, but they fell into the trap, given their concern about the ignorance of the laity, of identifying the liturgy essentially as a pattern of words. By the same token, they often lacked the historical knowledge of the context in which those words had come to life.

In the resulting sequence of verbal elements, the collect was simply the item which immediately preceded the reading of Scripture. As we observed earlier, Cranmer often retained the traditional collects of the Roman rite, which were a heritage from such collections as the Verona, Gelasian, and Gregorian sacramentaries. But when a collect seemed to suggest rejected teaching, such as the earning of merit, or a petition for the prayers of the saint of the day, in such instances either the text itself was modified or a new collect was written. It is in these latter cases that the collect was shaped with some clear connection to the readings which followed. One collect in particular stands out as an example of such a connection, and at the same time reflects the zeal of the Reformers for the reading of Scripture. The collect in question is the one Cranmer wrote for the second Sunday of Advent:

> Blessed lord, which hast caused all holy
> Scriptures to bee written for our learnyng;
> graunte us that we maye in suche wise heare
> them, read, marke, learne, and inwardly
> digeste them; that by pacience, and coum-
> fort of thy holy woorde, we may embrace,
> and euer holde fast the blessed hope of

euerlasting life, which thou hast geuen us in
our sauiour Jesus Christe.

The epistle which was read immediately after this collect
was Romans 15:4-13, which opened with the words:
"Whatsoever things were written aforetime were written
for our learning," so that the collect not only sounded the
theme of the reading, but also intensified its application
in the lives of the hearers.

This type of modification was not characteristic only
of the Anglican liturgy. Many of the collects used by
Lutherans were translations from the Latin repertory, but
in addition to these newer collects were written in a fuller
form which were specifically related to the appointed
readings. The most important author of these new
prayers was Veit Dietrich (1506-1549), who was a friend
of both Luther and Melancthon. These prayers were
known as "text collects" and intended for use from the
pulpit either before or after the sermon. Dietrich
composed some ninety-one collects. They eventually
attained a secure place in Lutheran worship in connection
either with the readings or with the sermon. The
influence of these collects was so great that Lutheran commentators on the liturgy came to understand the collect as
a preparation for the reading of Scripture.[16]

This connection between the collect and Scripture
came gradually to find uncritical acceptance similarly
among Anglican commentators, sometimes involving a
rereading of history which strikes us today as charming,
if somewhat naive. Charles Wheatley, for example, the
author of a commentary on the Book of Common Prayer
that was widely used during the eighteenth and nine-

teenth centuries, concludes a discussion of the collect with this comment: "I think it is very probable that the *collects for the Sundays and Holy-days* bear the name, upon account that a great many of them are very evidently collected out of the Epistles and Gospels."[17]

With the advent of serious historical study of the liturgy in connection with the Oxford Movement in the nineteenth century, such fantasy has had less influence and has certainly enjoyed less credence. The deepening of our historical insight into the origins and evolution of liturgical rites has prepared us for the liturgical changes of recent decades in which a rite is experienced not merely as a sequence of items but as the structuring of the common prayer of a community of faith and its commissioning to ministry in the world.

> Grant, O merciful God, that your Church, being gathered together in unity by your Holy Spirit, may show forth your power among all peoples, to the glory of your Name; through Jesus Christ our Lord, who lives and reigns with you and the Holy Spirit, one God, for ever and ever. *Amen.*
>
> (Collect for Proper 16)

Chapter Four

Using Words to Pray

Christian liturgical worship is more than words. It is a human event, a common action by a community of faith, which is rooted in and expressive of its identity in Christ. The understanding of corporate prayer that has been presented in these pages has thus placed the first priority in liturgical prayer upon the common faith which finds its public expression in the assembly of Christians. That faith is the interior energy of liturgical prayer. Without it, such prayer is meaningless.

At the center of faith there is the silence of awe before the Holy One, but because of the gift of speech, that awe presses toward articulation. Because we are, as human beings, drawn to communicate with others, that communication is potentially one of the most deeply human activities in which we participate. Words alone do not accomplish the full dimensions of personal communication, but they play an important role in it. Indifference to words leads along a path toward dehumanization, the impoverishment of a fundamental power with which we are endowed as humans.

So, in regard to the life of faith, words are critically important, not as an end in themselves but as signs of a wide world of meaning. We need words to point to realities which are beyond words alone to express. Words are one facet of a multivalent expression of meaning. In the liturgy, these various dimensions are held together in a creative encounter whose significance extends far beyond a merely didactic statement of theological truths.

Sacramental theologian Peter Fink has written of the three "languages" which come together in the Church's rites.[1] The first of these, the language of theology, in the strict sense has no place in the liturgical action. It is pre-liturgical. It is the language of theological reflection and instruction, rather like the question and answer language of a catechism. This is the language of an important aspect of Christian formation, of the Church's ministry of teaching. At the time of the Reformation, the Reformers introduced such language into the liturgy on a massive scale in reaction to the centuries-long failure of the Church to educate Christians for a mature life of faith. Although we may sympathize with the Reformers' recognition of the importance of this ministry of formation, its imposition upon the Church's sacramental rites was an inappropriate solution to the problem. For it implied that gathering for worship is primarily a verbal and cerebral experience. This attitude, combined with the fixity of texts made possible by the invention of printing a century prior to the Reformation, created an understanding of Christian worship which has dominated the liturgical practices of the Church in the centuries since that time. Such a view tends to see the Sunday assembly as the place where Christian truth is *taught* rather than where Christian faith is *celebrated*.

The other two "languages" of which Fink writes are directly related to the liturgical celebration. There is the language of prayer, of song, and of preaching. These are dimensions of a rite in which words are used — but for a celebrative rather than a didactic purpose. Even in the case of preaching, there is general agreement that the purpose of the sermon is best focused in the proclamation of the events of salvation history and not in moralistic instruction. The reading of Scripture and the sermon are thus in their way as truly a sacramental celebration as is the proclamation of the Eucharistic Prayer. In the sermon, and in the prayers and hymnody, words play an important role, but always as part of an experience which extends beyond the role of words alone. In regard to the collects, it is this aspect of liturgical langauge which will be examined here, but our discussion of the words we use in our forms of prayer must not lose sight of the third "language" of which Fink writes, and which he sees as "perhaps the most neglected of all." It is, he says, "the language of the event itself prior to and independent of the word which is proclaimed upon it. It is the language of space, of movement, of interaction. It speaks, expresses, and instructs as surely as do the other two."[2] Fink is making an important assertion here about the non-verbal dimensions of liturgical worship. Any discussion of the words that are used in the liturgical texts must involve an awareness of those aspects of corporate worship for which words are required, as well as those which stretch us beyond the capacity of words into the realm of sensual experience.

Anglican writers have often spoken of the power of liturgical rites to involve the whole person. There is, in other words, a physical engagement in the corporate liturgical action. Processions and other patterns of movement in the sanctuary evoke associations with a type of ritual dance. In some parishes, the use of incense and the involvement of the sense of smell has offered another dimension of non-verbal yet sensual participation. But it must be admitted that in many of the parishes which have been most characterized by an elaborate ritual tradition, this "language" has often been restricted to the sanctuary area and paralleled with an essentially passive piety of vision on the part of the laity in the pews. In other words, Fink's third language has found expression within the patterns of Anglican worship, but clerical domination of the rites has often left the laity with little more to do than to watch, firmly separated from the action and from each other by fixed pews. The non-verbal dimensions have not necessarily fostered the kind of personal interaction of which Fink writes. The negative reaction to the introduction of the Kiss of Peace into the eucharist of the Book of Common Prayer is a clear indication that personal interaction was not generally perceived as an appropriate corollary of the non-verbal dimensions of liturgical worship. Such physical touching was, and in some places continues to be, rejected as an intrusion into what was understood as the prayer of an individual worshiper.

Any discussion of the words used in the liturgical rites must involve this third language. When Fink speaks of "the language of the event prior to and independent of the word which is proclaimed upon it," he is placing the rite within the context of the Church's action and the Church's common act of faith. There the individual believers must come to understand themselves as involved in a model of prayer which is essentially corporate, that is, in which the whole assembly of believers is involved as a community of faith and not as a convenient gathering of individuals.

This fuller framework of liturgical prayer suggests the fundamental error of various publications of the Society for the Preservation of the Book of Common Prayer, which were highly critical of the new texts which have been introduced into the 1979 Book of Common Prayer. It will be obvious from comments at the beginning of this chapter that stewardship of the language of prayer is a significant responsibility in the Church, but critics of the new texts have spoken of liturgical texts as though they were the whole of the matter. Yet liturgy is more than the second language discussed earlier, namely, the words of prayer-texts, hymnody and preaching. When we discover that the third language "speaks, expresses, and instructs as surely as do the other two," such a narrow identification of liturgy with certain hallowed texts becomes absurd.

In an essay entitled "Modern Translations of the Bible," C. S. Lewis warns us about this kind of textual idolatry in words that apply equally to an excessive attachment to the beautiful texts and earlier versions of the Prayer Book. Lewis writes,

> We must sometimes get away from the Authorized Version, if for no other reason, simply *because* it is so beautiful and so solemn. Beauty exalts, but beauty also lulls. Early associations endear but they also confuse. Through that beautiful solemnity the transporting or horrifying realities of which the Book tells may come to us blunted and disarmed and we may only sigh with tranquil veneration when we ought to be burning with shame or struck dumb with terror or carried out of ourselves by ravishing hopes and adorations.[3]

These words are a powerful caution to any inclination on our part to make the text an end in itself. The life of faith to which Christ calls the members of his Body is not the result of using language which sounds religious any more than it is a matter of worshipping in a building which "looks like a church." Such emphasis upon the external aspects of worship, whether verbal or non-verbal, fails to grasp the fundamental relation of faith to the transformation of life style.

The use of the most holy language to be found in the entire liturgical tradition does not guarantee the living of a holy life. Without adequate Christian formation (that is, Fink's pre-liturgical first language) it can even lull us into a confusion between the outer forms and the realities of an authentically Christian life-style. The common failure among well-intentioned Christians to make connections between what is prayed in the liturgy and what is lived in daily life is a constant reminder of our failure to deal adequately in adult formation with the pre-liturgical aspects of Christian faith. Christian liturgical prayer, encompassing both its verbal and non-verbal dimensions, always presumes an active faith in the lives of participants. Without the Church's prioritization of mature formation in faith, it becomes all too easy for Christian practice to focus on these external dimensions in apparent ignorance of the foundation upon which they depend. Neither an intellectual nor an aesthetic experience may, for the Christian, be substituted for the commitment of faith, yet both may serve to nourish that faith.

To raise this concern for the pre-liturgical aspects of ministry does not mean that our stewardship of the words we use in prayer is unimportant. As corporate event, as the common experience of what we proclaim to be the source of our life and our salvation, the words we say about God and the words we address to God in liturgical prayer are inevitably linked to the process within the Church by which those words are chosen and eventually authorized as the basis of the Church's common prayer. The issue which faces us in this process is whether it is appropriate for the language of ordinary life to be used as the language of liturgical prayer.

The liturgical rites which emerged at the time of the Reformation were based upon the use of the vernacular as a matter of principle, but this tended to be a vernacular of an elevated style. It eventually became as fixed in use as had been the Latin of medieval Catholicism. The new liturgical rites of the recent revisions have had to grapple with this question more strenuously than before because of the increased pressure at the pastoral level for the use of a more contemporary style of language in liturgical prayer. The American Book of Common Prayer of 1979 is a transitional document in this regard, both preserving the traditional style and also supplying modern language forms for such basic rites as Morning and Evening Prayer and the Holy Eucharist. Of special interest for this study is the inclusion of all the collects in both styles of language. In spite of critics, however, it is generally agreed that the modern forms at their best achieve that quailty of *distance* from the language of every day which responds to the solemn character of public liturgical prayer, and which is clearly one of the qualities of the traditional forms. The images of these modern forms are experienced as closer to the life we live; thus they save us from an excessive distancing which many feel when the traditional forms, in spite of their literary beauty, are used. It has been the excessive formalism of the traditional language which has generated the imperative for a new vocabulary of prayer that is clearly related to the world in which we find ourselves and reflects our own experience.

In spite of this contemporary pastoral imperative, it must be acknowledged that the body of collects preserved in the Prayer Book tradition is a remarkable collection of prayers, characterized by those qualities of simplicity and restraint which were characteristic of the classical Latin collects. Although Archbishop Cranmer reworked the Latin collects, rather than merely translating them, the results were on the whole worthy of comparison to the original Latin forms. In connection with the problems of translation or of new composition today, it is important to recall Cranmer's debt to the body of Latin collects that are one of the glories of the Western liturgical tradition.

Anyone who has undertaken a work of translation knows how difficult it is to realize in the second language the stylistic characteristics of the first, yet we find in Cranmer's work a similar tightness of structure to that which is found in the Latin forms. One particularly fine example is the collect long associated for Anglicans with the fourteenth Sunday after Trinity, and now appointed as the collect for Proper 25. The Latin original reads:

> *Omnipotens sempiterne Deus, da nobis fidei,*
> *spei et caritatis augmentum: et, ut mereamur*
> *assequi quod promittis, fac nos amare quod*
> *praecipis.*

Cranmer's version is both a translation and a theological modification. In the Book of Common Prayer of 1549, it reads:

> Almightye and euerlastyng God, geue unto
> us the increase of faythe, hope, and charitie;
> and that we may obteine that whiche thou
> doest promise; make us to loue that which
> thou doest commaunde.

The translation into English obviously requires more words, but the result is still succinct in style. Cranmer's theological modification is seen in his rejection of the phrase "ut mereamur assequi quod promittis," ("that we may deserve to obtain what you promise") for "that we may obteine that which thou doest promise," and thus to remove any idea of merit from the prayer. This theological issue will be considered later.

The late English actor Robert Speaight, a Roman Catholic layman who was deeply concerned about the quality of language used in the liturgy, commented in an article entitled "Liturgy and Language" that Cranmer's worst pain in our contemporary situation "would surely be the knowledge of how atrociously the Roman Catholics of today have translated the prayers which he once translated so sublimely."[4] The difficulty of translation into the contemporary idiom is immediately evident when we consider the first authorized version of the above collect which was prepared by the International Committee on English in the Liturgy (ICEL) for use in the Roman rite for the Sixteenth Sunday in Ordinary Time:

> Lord, be merciful to your people. Fill us
> with your gifts and make us always eager to
> serve you in faith, hope, and love.

The impoverishment of the Latin form is obvious, and the theological modification makes that of Cranmer appear modest indeed. This example is given not as a condemnation of the work of ICEL: ample criticism has already emerged from within the Roman Church.[5] The example serves rather as a sign of the enormous difficulty posed by the translation or composition of collects for use in a liturgical rite celebrated in a contemporary idiom. To get to this problem, it would perhaps be useful here to consider the characteristics of the original Latin forms.

Earlier I observed that in the Roman rite, the prayer which concludes the entrance is known simply as *oratio*, that is, "prayer." We have suggested that our term "collect" has its origin in the gathering of the faithful at an appointed location, known as a "station." The classical collect form which we have associated especially with the liturgical writings of Leo the Great is designated as *oratio* in the Roman liturgical documents. As a literary piece its content and style merit special discussion, since it is this Latin form that is the immediate source of the collect as it has developed within the Anglican liturgical tradition.

The *oratio* of the Roman rite is, in its Latin forms, an example of proclaimed public prayer that links us to the early tradition of improvised liturgical prayer. The word itself — *oratio* — can be misleading, evoking a possible association with "oration," a declamatory address or a speech. Yet Christine Mohrmann, a respected authority on liturgical Latin, connects the word rather with *orare*, "to pray," seeing the collect as immediately linked to the *oremus* — "let us pray" — of the eucharistic celebrant. Yet, in spite of her rejection of a declamatory sense to the form, Mohrmann sees the sources of the collect style in the pre-Christian rhetorical tradition of Rome. The succinct phrases of the collect are indicative, she believes, of "the style processes of the art of polished speech, taught and practice for centuries in the schools of Rome."[6] The form is truly classical in the sense that it is an example of a general pattern of prayer, not limited to a Christian context, in which an invocation addressed to God is followed by a relative clause that describes some aspect of the divine activity. In turn, this provides the

[97]

foundation for the petition which follows. It is a pattern that corresponds to that discussed in the second chapter of this book as the form of the liturgical collect.

In the early stages of preparation for a revision of the American Book of Common Prayer, the Standing Liturgical Commission stated the principles upon which new translations of the collects would be based. In this connection, the determinative impact of Cranmer's work for the Prayer Book tradition was acknowledged from the outset.

> Those who are most versed in the Latin Collects recognize how difficult they are to translate into modern vernaculars with the precision and rhythm of the originals. The achievement of Archbishop Cranmer in this respect has been universally applauded, and his style and method have served as a classic model both for translating the Collects and for composing new ones on the ancient pattern. The Collect is nonetheless a complicated sentence of a particular Latin style of rhetoric. Even the best ones require concentrated attention, repetition, and reflection, whether by hearing or by reading, to savor their full meaning and implication.[7]

Thus, the approach toward revision of the collects for the American Prayer Book was quite different from that of ICEL with its rejection of the literary formalism associated, for example, with the use of the relative clause. The method of the Standing Liturgical Commission was clearly within the tradition established by Cranmer but, in the contemporary translations, it incorporated necessary modernization of both grammar and vocabulary. As the Commission noted, "Every revision of the Prayer Book has exhibited modifications and refinements of the Collects, if only to bring them more nearly into line with the changing vernacular."[8]

By way of example, we may consider a sequence of translations and modifications in the forms of one specific collect, that for the Sunday of the Passion, or Palm Sunday, designated by Cranmer simply as the Sunday next before Easter. In its original Latin form, the collect reads:

> *Omnipotens sempiterne Deus, qui humano generi, ad imitandum humilitatis exemplum, Salvatorem nostrum carnem sumere et crucem subire fecisti: concede propitius, ut et patientiae ipsius habere documenta, et resurrectionis consortia mereamur. Per eumdem Dominum . . . .*

We get a sense of the difficulty of translation of this prayer into English if we compare it first of all to a literal translation, or at least as literal a translation as is possible if the new version is to be recognizable as acceptable English use. A literal version might read:

> Almighty everlasting God, who sent our Savior to the human race to take flesh and to submit to the cross, so that we might imitate the example of his humility:

mercifully grant that we might merit both to
have the proofs of his patience and a share
in his resurrection. Through the same Jesus
Christ our Lord . . . .

It is immediately obvious that this is not a modernized
version of the translation or adaptation of the prayer that
Archbishop Cranmer prepared for the Prayer Book of
1549, for it evokes nothing of the inner rhythm and
beauty of language which are characteristic both of the
Latin original and of Cranmer's work. It is quite
precisely *literal*: it is a flat translation which supplies the
sense of the text, but none of its literary subtlety. As
Stella Brook has commented in her study of the language
of the Prayer Book, "What is required, linguistically,
from an English Book of Common Prayer is not an
impeccable rendering of a Latin source, but a use of the
natural potentialities of English as full and satisfying as
the use made of the natural potentialities of Latin in a
Latin liturgy."[9] This is precisely what was required in
the preparation of a vernacular liturgy at the time of the
Reformation, a task for which Thomas Cranmer was
providentially gifted.

When we consider Cranmer's version of the Latin
collect, we find tangible proof of his achievement. The
text in the 1549 Book of Common Prayer reads:

Almightie and euerlastynge God, which of
thy tender loue towarde man, haste sent our
sauior Jesus Christ, to take upon him oure
fleshe, and to suffre death upon the crosse,
that all mankynde shoulde folowe the

example of his greate humilitie; mercifully graunte that we both folowe the example of his pacience, and be made partakers of his resurreccion; thoroughe the same Jesus Christ our lorde . . . .

This version by Cranmer has undergone only modest change over the centuries, and now appears in the American Book of Common Prayer essentially as Cranmer wrote it, but with modified spelling, as follows:

Almighty and everlasting God, who, of thy tender love towards mankind, hast sent thy Son our Savior Jesus Christ to take upon him our flesh, and to suffer death upon the cross, that all mankind should follow the example of his great humility: Mercifully grant that we may both follow the example of his patience, and also be made partakers of his resurrection; through the same Jesus Christ our Lord . . . .

When we compare either of the last two, almost identical, versions with the literal translation given earlier, we are confronted with radically contrasting levels of literary quality. Much of what distinguishes the Cranmerian version is simply the sensitivity to the rhythm of the English language. The phrases of the literal version are brief, even abrupt, comparable to the terseness which is characteristic of Latin. For this collect to work in English, a filling-out is required, not only of words but of images. The result in Cranmer's version is not a greatly increased length, but only what is felt to be necessary for the appropriate expression of the central ideas of the orginal Latin form.

Changes in Cranmer's translations from the Latin are not limited to the requirements of an English style. Matters of doctrine are also a factor in certain of the collects, including the one we are considering. The primary theological issue of the Reformation was the doctrine of justification by faith. Many of the earliest Latin collects similarly insist upon the absolute primacy of God's grace, thus they reflect an Augustinian theology in accord with the concern of the Reformers that salvation is God's gift, and not something which is earned through merit on the part of the believer. Any reference to *merit*, however, was sure to trigger suspicion on the part of any child of the Reformation. Thus the word *mereamur* which occurs in the Latin version of our collect could not find a place in Cranmer's version. "Grant that we might merit" becomes in the 1549 Prayer Book "graunte that we both folowe," so that Christ becomes the example of those virtues which the Church prays may be mirrored in the lives of the faithful. Later in this chapter we shall see how this concern about "merit" will affect the way Cranmer deals with the collects for the feasts of saints. Now let us consider one further stage in the evolution of the collect for the Sunday prior to Easter, the contemporary form in the 1979 Book of Common Prayer.

The problem before us in this last example is the challenge of a translation into a modern English idiom. We have observed in Cranmer's work an adaptation of the Latin form, where a modest enlargement incorporates the primary images of the original collect in a genuinely English form of expression. Cranmer accomplished this without landing in the lengthy verbal patterns which are characteristic of many post-Reformation forms of prayer. This is the problem which confronted ICEL in its preparation of translations of the collects for the new Roman missal. The complex relative clauses that characterize the Latin forms, and which Cranmer reshaped in the English versions, are not at home in modern English, whether spoken or written. This raises the question as to whether the form is even viable for use in a liturgical rite which uses contemporary language.

The solution taken by ICEL in the first stage of its work was to break up the Latin versions into two or three sentences, and thus to avoid the relative clause. The Standing Liturgical Commission decided to retain the classical form but also seek to modernize the Cranmerian style, and thus achieve needed change while maintaining continuity within the Anglican liturgical tradition. What they have sought for is a living liturgical style which incorporates the rhythms of the language of today and yet evokes the great heritage of Prayer Book workship. The contemporary form of the collect we have been considering reads as follows:

> Almighty and everliving God, in your tender love for the human race you sent your Son our Savior Jesus Christ to take upon him our nature, and to suffer death upon the cross, giving us the example of his great humility: Mercifully grant that we may walk in the way of his suffering, and

[103]

> also share in his resurrection; through Jesus
> Christ our Lord . . . .

The essential conservatism of this version, reflected in the decision to adhere to the classical form, is all the more obvious if we consider it in comparison with the ICEL collect for the same eucharist.

> Almighty, ever-living God, you have given the human race Jesus Christ our Savior as a model of humility. He fulfilled your will by becoming man and giving his life on the cross. Help us to bear witness to you by following his example of suffering and make us worthy to share in his resurrection. We ask this through our Lord Jesus Christ . . . .

The new Prayer Book version is one extended complex sentence. Although somewhat longer than the Latin version, it is structurally closely akin to it. The ICEL version, on the other hand, is, apart from the concluding doxology, made up of three separate sentences. Richard Toporoski has voiced the criticism of ICEL's translations that they replace "religious English" with contemporary colloquial speech.[10] Yet neither of these two contemporary versions uses archaic language. Both employ a vocabulary which can be found in contemporary speech. The final effect in each example is, however, quite different. Although I would want to avoid a narrow, sectarian bias, the Prayer Book version seems to reflect that quality of *distance* which separates ritual language from merely colloquial use. The contrast is similar to that between poetry and prose in achieving their purpose. Both prayers are saying essentially the same thing, but in clearly distinct ways.

Concerning the Prayer Book version, there are those who would argue that the desired distancing of ritual prayer is undermined by the adjustment to modern forms, the substitution, for example, of "your" for "thy." Leonel Mitchell has spoken to this concern by noting that the use of "thou" in sixteenth century English had the opposite effect from that for which advocates would see such forms used today.[11] "Thou" was not a formal address, but rather more intimate or familiar than "you." The 1979 Prayer Book, as we have noted, supplies both traditional and contemporary versions of all the collects, which allows for a helpful pastoral flexibility during a time of transition. The modernization of such forms, however, does not affect the character of the contemporary version to any serious degree. The distancing without the loss of intelligibility which many feel should characterize formal liturgical prayer is much more a matter of sentence structure than of the use or non-use of archaic words.

The distinctions between the two contemporary forms come down to a question of literary nuance. The rhythms of the two prayers are different, and yet both employ a basic English vocabulary. The rhythm of the ICEL version is akin to that of colloquial speech, as was the intention of the Commission. The Prayer Book version, by contrast, while expressing the same ideas, uses an English syntax which is more removed from ordinary conversational patterns.

It is interesting to note that both versions have used the words "human race," which is faithful to the original Latin, but is indicative within the Prayer Book tradition of a move toward inclusive language in place of male-imaged nouns and pronouns. Previous Prayer Book versions had used either "man" or "mankind" at this point. Yet in their references to the Incarnation, there is a notable contrast between the two forms: the Prayer Book version speaks of Christ taking "our nature," whereas the ICEL text speaks of his "becoming man." In this instance, the Prayer Book is closer to the Latin which refers to "our flesh" in an inclusive rather than exclusive reference.

The Prayer Book version also preserves an addition to the collect which Cranmer inserted into the 1549 form. The words "which of thy tender love" make a gentle shift from the Latin version. In the orginal form, God is acknowledged as the one who sent the Savior to the human race. Cranmer enlarged the phrase by referring to God's love "toward man." This seems to be more than merely an expansion to accord with English literary style. It suggests a theological concern. The Latin form refers, of course, to Christ's humility, but in Cranmer's version, the reference to God's love as the motivating energy of the Incarnation seems to be a complement to that quality in Christ, imaging the Father not as a remote ruler but as one disposed in love toward the creation. In this perspective, it is interesting to note Massey Shepherd's comment on this collect, that it is "the nearest thing to a statement of the doctrine of Atonement to be found in the Prayer Book, and it is significant that it associates it with Christ's Incarnation no less than his Passion."[12]

What, then, Cranmer accomplished in the addition of these few words, is to mirror the love of God in the birth and death of Christ.

The theology of the Atonement appears even more prominently in the alternative prayer which appears in the Roman Missal for Passion Sunday. The alternative versions were prepared by ICEL as new compositions, although clearly related in theme to the collect that is directly adapted from the Latin version. The text of the alternative prayer reads:

> Almighty Father of our Lord Jesus Christ, you sent your Son to be born of woman and to die on a cross, so that through the obedience of one man, estrangement might be dissolved for all men. Guide our minds by his truth and strengthen our lives by the example of his death, that we may live in union with you in the kingdom of your promise. Grant this through Christ our Lord.

The syntax of this prayer is more complex than that of the first version, so that there is a better sense of movement within the flow of the language. Although it is not really successful, it is a useful example of experimentation with a somewhat richer texture than that of its companion. What is particularly interesting from an Anglican perspective is to note the theological substance of the prayer. There was perhaps no conscious link with the emphasis in Cranmer which was noted above, but it is quite evident that a clearly-articulated theology of the

Atonement has found a home in this alternative form. The birth and death of Christ are directly linked to God's purpose of ending the estrangement between mankind and God. In accord with Massey Shepherd's comment quoted earlier on the Prayer Book version, the prayer thus associates the Atonement "with Christ's Incarnation no less than his Passion."

Although we shall be considering the theology of the collects more fully in the final chapter, it is important to note that we cannot radically separate matters of theology from the issue of language. The liturgy has a formative impact on the theological perceptions of the gathered faithful, but not in terms of what Peter Fink calls the *first* language of sacramental rites, that is, the language of instruction. As I noted earlier, the language of catechesis is more appropriately pre-liturgical. Yet liturgical experience is still theologically formative in the line of Fink's *second* language, the language of rite and song, in which faith is celebrated by the community which shares that common faith and is thereby formed more deeply by it. The Atonement theology of Cranmer's collect, or as it is expressed in the alternative Roman form, does not touch us as instruction but as proclamation. It lifts up before the assembly the faith into which they have been baptized, and thus shapes them by evoking the images of the mystery of God's act into which their lives have been grafted. The language of liturgical prayer is thus a matter of the greatest importance, and not merely or even primarily for literary purists. The texts are icons, patterns of words, which not only state but symbolize, participate in the reality of, what they proclaim.

*   *   *   *

I have considered the collect for Passion Sunday in detail as an example that links the evolution of the collect in the Prayer Book tradition with its Latin origins. The collection of collects in the 1979 Book of Common Prayer amply demonstrates the continued value of the ancient Latin prayers as a resource for liturgical prayer today. The *Commentary on the American Prayer Book* by Marion J. Hatchett gives detailed information about the origins or authorship of each collect, and it is remarkable what a large percentage, often in adaptation as well as translation, come down to us from one or another of the ancient collections of Latin liturgical texts known as a *sacramentary*.[13] Some of the collects that are new to the Prayer Book expand the use of such Latin resources beyond that of the 1549 Book of Common Prayer. One example of such a collect, new to the Prayer Book but based upon an ancient Latin form, is the collect for Thursday in Easter Week. Not only does the prayer appear in both traditional and contemporary forms, but it is also appointed for use at the Easter Vigil as well as on the Second Sunday of Easter. It is a remarkably fine prayer, which unites images of baptismal rebirth and fellowship in the Church to the Paschal celebration as the foundation of the new covenant. From this material flows the petition of the collect that all the baptized "may show forth in their lives what they profess by their faith," in other words, that the fruit of the baptismal covenant be found in a transformed life-style. Although the theological substance of the collect is quite rich, it is not heavily didactic, but rather demonstrates that almost poetic quality found in the greatest of the collects. The full text of the Prayer Book version reads:

> Almighty and Everlasting God, who in the Paschal mystery established the new covenant of reconciliation: Grant that all who have been reborn into the fellowship of Christ's Body may show forth in their lives what they profess by their faith; through Jesus Christ our Lord . . . .

The original Latin form of this prayer appears in a document known as the Gregorian Sacramentary, a collection of liturgical texts which were assembled at Rome in about the year 595 A.D. The Latin text is a tightly expressed example of the classical form:

> *Omnipotens sempiterne Deus, qui paschale sacramentum in reconciliationis humanae foedere contulisti: da mentibus nostris, ut, quod professione celebramus, imitemur effectu. Per Dominum . . . .*[14]

Once again, the Prayer Book version offers a theologically enriched form of this prayer with its reference to being "reborn into the fellowship of Christ's Body," that is, in uniting membership in the Church to the reference to the Paschal mystery. By way of comparison, the ICEL version of the Latin collect, appointed for Friday in Easter week, reads as follows:

> Eternal Father, you gave us the Easter

mystery as our covenant of reconciliation.
May the new birth we celebrate show its
effects in the way we live. We ask this
through our Lord Jesus Christ . . . .

Once again, the literal sense of the original is given in
this translation, but it lacks not only the theological richness which we have noted in the Prayer Book version, but
also its rhythmic subtlety as well.

Another collect from the Latin sources that is new to
the Prayer Book is the first alternative collect appointed
for the feast of Pentecost. The text is found in another
of the sixth century sacramentaries, the Gelasian, where it
is given as a second collect for Pentecost.[15] Marion
Hatchett's *Commentary* supplies a translation of the Latin
version, which serves as an interesting basis of comparison to both the Prayer Book and ICEL versions:

God, who on this festal day sanctified your
universal church for every race and nation:
Pour out through the whole world the gifts
of your Holy Spirit, that what was begun
among them at the beginning of the
preaching of the Gospel with divine
magnanimity may now also be poured out
through the hearts of believers.[16]

The reference to the account of the event of Pentecost as
reported in Acts 2 contributes to the complexity of this
prayer. The Prayer Book version, although clearly based
upon the Gelasian form, involves considerable adaptation
of the original. It reads:

> Almighty God, on this day you opened the
> way of eternal life to every race and nation
> by the promised gift of your Holy Spirit:
> Shed abroad this gift throughout the world
> by the preaching of the Gospel, that it may
> reach to the ends of the earth; through Jesus
> Christ our Lord . . . .

Although the ICEL version is quite different, it is closer
to the Latin in preserving the reference to the Holy Spirit
as working "through the hearts of believers," which does
not appear in the above Prayer Book form. Nevertheless,
the ICEL version again reflects a rather radical simplification of the ancient form. It is diminished by the lack
of a clear connection with the description of the
Pentecost event in Acts, resulting in an impoverished
adaptation of the Latin. The ICEL text reads:

> God our Father, let the Spirit you sent on
> your Church to begin the teaching of the
> gospel continue to work in the world
> through the hearts of all who believe. We
> ask this through our Lord Jesus Christ . . . .

It is interesting to note that the contemporary version of
the Prayer Book does not include the relative clause of
the Latin version, which continued as a characteristic of
most of Cranmer's translations and is retained in the
traditional Prayer Book form. In this example, the
contemporary Prayer Book form seems to have been
shaped by the same kind of concern we find in the ICEL
versions — a concern about modern styles of expression.

On the whole, both contemporary versions are far more adaptations than translations.

In addition to new material from Latin sources, either translated or adapted, the 1979 Book of Common Prayer also includes newly-written collects prepared specifically for this edition of the Prayer Book. Massey H. Shepherd, Jr., who served as Vice-Chairman of the Standing Liturgical Commission during the preparation of the new book, and who was for many years a major influence in liturgical studies as well as Prayer Book revision, had a prominent role in the shaping of the new collection of collects. One of his own compositions is that appointed for the Fifth Sunday after the Epiphany, which reads:

> Set us free, O God, from the bondage of our sins, and give us the liberty of that abundant life which you have made known to us in your Son our Savior Jesus Christ; who lives . . . .

The new collect is rich in scriptural allusions, as Hatchett observes,[17] but the allusions are not to passages among those appointed for that Sunday in any of the three cycles of the Prayer Book lectionary. It is not related to the readings which follow it, but rather is a general collect that draws upon biblical images. Although it abbreviates the form of the classical pattern, the collect displays those literary qualities which have characterized its diverse expressions in the Prayer Book tradition. Its focused structure makes it worthy of comparison with those Latin examples whose concentration is akin to that of great poetry.

[113]

*   *   *   *

While Archbishop Cranmer used the Latin sources for many of his collects for the Sundays of the year, translating or adapting them according to his purposes, this was not the case when he came to the collects for saints' days. The reason for this was mentioned earlier in reference to our discussion of the collect for the Sunday of the Passion. Cranmer was deeply influenced by the theological principles of the continental Reformers, and to him it was quite unacceptable that collects which asked for or referred to the prayers of the saints should be preserved within a reformed liturgical tradition. A consistent principle in Cranmer's work on the collects for the cycle of saints' days, it has remained a constant in the writing of such collects for later editions of the Book of Common Prayer.

The Reformers rejected the idea of the intercessory power of the saints, an idea drawn from the concept of a privileged status enjoyed by the departed saints on the basis of their merits. For the Reformers, *all* merit was found in Christ alone. Prayer based upon some supposed merit of the saints suggested an insufficiency in the merit of the cross, and was thus deemed unbiblical and a theological error.

For saints' days, whenever Cranmer used a Latin collect as a source, any reference to intercession was removed along with any comments on the particular saint's merits. Cranmer preferred to draw upon some incident in the saint's life or some pious quality associated with the saint that provided an example and model for later Christians. The evolution of the collect for the feast of St. Andrew (November 30) offers us a good example of Cranmer's method. In the original Latin form, which is found in the Gelasian Sacramentary, the text asks that Andrew "may be to us a perpetual intercessor."[18] Such a phrase was, of course, intolerable for the Archbishop's use, and he prepared a new collect for the 1549 Prayer Book, based upon a legend about Andrew's death:

> Almightie God, whiche haste geuen suche grace to thy Apostle saincte Andrewe, that he counted the sharp and painful death of the crosse to be an high honour, and a great glory: Graunt vs to take and esteme al troubles and aduersities which shall come vnto vs for thy sake, as thinges profitable for vs toward the obtayning of euerlasting lyfe: through Iesus Christe our Lorde.

Only a short time afterwards, when Cranmer prepared for the 1552 Book, St. Andrew's was the only collect which was replaced. This was probably due to a conviction that even legendary material has no place in Christian worship. The collect for the 1552 Book, although related to the earlier version in its opening phrase, is essentially a new prayer, based upon the biblical story of Andrew's call. The text reads:

> Almightie God which didst geue such grace vnto thy holy Apostle Saincte Andrewe, that he redily obeyed the callyng of thy sone Iesus Christ, and followed hym without

[115]

> delaye: Graunte vnto vs all, that we being
> called by the holy worde, may furthwith
> geue ouer our selfes, obediently to folow thy
> holy commaundements: through the same
> Iesus Chryste our Lorde.

This shift in the two Cranmerian Prayer Books is typical of his general approach to the place of the saints in the liturgy, beginning with the 1549 Book. Apart from feasts of our Lord, special commemorations were limited to the apostles, the evangelists, St. Stephen, the Holy Innocents, St. Michael and all Angels, and the feast of All Saints. In effect, Cranmer tended to limit the saints to those whose names appear in the New Testament. The Reformation principle of *Scripture alone* thus had very direct impact upon the shaping of the cycle of saints' days as it found a place in the Book of Common Prayer. This excluded, of course, a large number of saints who were the focus of much popular piety in the late medieval period, but it was a convenient rule by which to abolish superstitious devotion that placed saints into the mediatorial role of Christ. In his liturgical work, Cranmer thus represents the general realization among the Reformers that the Church had lost a sense of the primacy of Scripture and of the unique role of Jesus Christ as proclaimed in that Scripture.

The attitude toward the role of the saints which is indicated in Cranmer's manner of redoing the collects for their feasts reveals a shift to an attitude which was prevalent during the first three centuries of the Church, that is, prior to the liberation of the Church by Constantine in the fourth century. Anglican liturgy honors the saints not as intercessors, but as *examples*. This attitude was classically stated by Jeremy Taylor a century after Cranmer; in an apologetical pamphlet written in response to Puritan opposition, he supports the use of liturgical forms:

> If we delight to remember those holy persons whose bodies rest in the bed of peace and whose souls are deposited in the hands of Christ till the day of restitution of all things, we may, by the collects and days of anniversary-festivity, not only remember, but also imitate them too in our lives, if we will make that use of the proportions of Scripture allotted for the festival which the Church intends.[19]

The idea that Christians are called to imitate the saints implies a quite different attitude from that in which the saints are seen as intermediaries whose virtues make their prayers more "worthy" than those of ordinary Christians. The saint as an *example* to ordinary Christians is the principle upon which Prayer Book collects for saints' days are based. Christians are to imitate the saints.

Such a principle is evident not only in Cranmer's 1552 collect for St. Andrew, but also in his collect for St. Matthias (February 24). This collect has a dual reference: Judas is an example of a false apostle whereas Matthias, by implication, is an example of a faithful and true pastor. The idea of imitation is made explicit in the collect for St. Joseph (March 19), which is a new addition to the cycle of saints in the American Prayer Book. The text asks God to "give us grace to imitate his uprightness of life and his obedience to your commands." The principle is again explicit in the collect for St. Barnabas (June 11), which begins, "Grant, O God, that we may follow the example of your faithful servant Barnabas." In these collects and in the Anglican cycle of saints' collects as a whole, the principle remains intact: the saints are exemplars of the faith, those who exemplify the virtues which all Christians are called to in daily life. This fundamental perspective is summed up in the first of the common collects appointed for the commemoration "Of a Saint":

> Almighty God, you have surrounded us with
> a great cloud of witnesses: Grant that we,
> encouraged by the good example of your
> servant N., may persevere in running the
> race that is set before us, until at last we
> may with *him* attain to your eternal joy;
> through Jesus Christ . . . .

The collect evokes the opening verses of Hebrews 12, and is expressive of the attitude toward the saints which was common in the church of the early centuries.

It is interesting to note that the third of the common collects for a saint is a newly-composed prayer which sees us as "surrounded by their witness," as has been characteristic of the collects we have considered. But this new collect also asks "that in our earthly pilgrimage we may always be supported by this fellowship of love and prayer." This latter phrase is, of course, a considerable distance removed from the "Pray for us" which was so abhorrent to the sixteenth-century reformers, and it strongly suggests our sharing with the saints in the common life of the Body of Christ. Today, far removed from the polarized positions taken at the Reformation, is it possible to imagine that this is a reference to the prayers of the saints of which Cranmer would have approved?

Among the new collects for use on saints' days in the Episcopal Church are those authorized for what are known as "lesser feasts." These are commemorations of a wide range of persons who are remembered as important examples of Christian virtue or courage, but which are not proposed in the Book of Common Prayer as Principal Feasts or Holy Days that have a universal signficance for the whole Church. In other words, the Prayer Book clearly intends that such major days deserve a priority of place in the liturgical cycle of the Christian Year. Lesser feasts are supplied with collect, psalm, and Scripture readings, but it is evident that there is a certain optional character in regard to their observance.[20]

The liturgical materials supplied in *Lesser Feasts and Fasts* are the fruit of about two decades of evolution in the use of the Episcopal Church. The first two editions, of 1964 and 1973, were authorized by the General Convention only for trial use; the third edition is authorized for optional use without a limit of time. For the sake of convenience, the volume also includes the Prayer Book materials for the major holy days. All the commemorations, whether categorized as major or minor, are preceded by notes which illuminate some aspects of the commemoration, as well as biographical information about the saint who is being commemorated. This material is useful for teaching purposes since many of these heroes of the faith who are being held up as examples to the Church today are, in fact, often quite unfamiliar to contemporary Christians.

The collects for such lesser feasts were written so that each collect would include some distinctive association with the particular saint. In several instances this is accomplished through a quotation of the very words of the saint. In the collect of Jeremy Taylor, whose support for such commemorations was quoted above, phrases from a prayer which he wrote are incorporated into a reference to Taylor himself. Similarly, in the collect for Richard of Chichester, the saint's well-known petition to Christ that he might "see thee more clearly, love thee more dearly, and follow thee more nearly" becomes the petition asked by the Church itself as it commemorates the saint.[21]

In some of the collects these allusions have an amusing ring, not so much when they involve a direct quotation from the writings of the saint but rather when they belabor a point in an attempt to teach a lesson. The collect for Thomas Bray, who founded the Society for Promoting Christian Knowledge and the Society for the Propagation of the Gospel, offers such an example:

> O God of compassion, you opened the eyes of your servant Thomas Bray to see the needs of the Church in the New World, and led him to found societies to meet those needs: Make the Church in this land diligent at all times to *propagate the Gospel* among those who have not received it, and to *promote* the spread of *Christian know-*

ledge; through Jesus Christ our Lord . . . .[22]

Such literalisms have a heavily didactic ring. One sees here a tendency to try to have the collect *teach* the story of the saint rather than to celebrate it. Given the unfamilarity of many of these commemorated heroes, this didactic use is an easy temptation, but really requires deeper attention in some other way.

The newly-authorized collect for Martin Luther King, Jr. also takes a familiar phrase associated with King into his collect, but in so doing runs the risk of turning it into a cliché. The collect begins, "O Saving God, by the hand of Moses your servant you led your people out of slavery, and made them *free at last* . . . ."[23] The problem here is not the parallel between Moses and King which it suggests, but rather the reading backward in time of a phrase — "free at last" — strongly rooted in the identity not of Moses but of Martin Luther King. One is left with a potentially ludicrous juxtaposition, which could have been avoided with a more encompassing reference to the *freedom* to which both men called their people.

Such a criticism, however, is not intended to detract from the operative principle which has characterized the Anglican tradition of collects for saints and which continues in the 1979 Prayer Book. The saints are not only examples to us, they are also persons rooted in history like ourselves, living heroic lives in the face of challenges similar to those of our own life. They are thus abiding witnesses of a God who continues to act in human history, and who will use even our gifts for the purposes of redemption.

[121]

Almighty and everliving God, whose servant Thomas Cranmer, with others, restored the language of the people in the prayers of your Church: Make us always thankful for this heritage; and help us so to pray in the Spirit and with the understanding, that we may worthily magnify your holy Name; through Jesus Christ our Lord, who lives and reigns with you and the Holy Spirit, one God, for ever and ever. *Amen.*

(Collect to commemorate The
First Book of Common Prayer)

Chapter Five

Theology Prayed

During the recent decades of liturgical renewal, many writers have had occasion to refer to an ancient adage concerning the relation between the prayer of the Church and its faith which affirms that "the law of prayer establishes the law of faith." This phrase has been explored almost to excess, and yet its significance is such that we must also consider it here. This is a book about the prayer of the Christian community, and if the adage is as significant as recent writings imply, then the prayer of the community is the primary expression of the faith of the community.[1]

One of the significant after-effects of the Protestant Reformation upon worship was, as a dimension of the reemphasis of the Word of God in the Christian life, a concern for the didactic potential of liturgial rites. The Christian assembly came to be understood preeminently in terms of the opportunity it offered for the teaching of the faith. There is no question that the didactic aspects of Christian formation had been seriously ignored during the centuries prior to the Reformation, but the accomplishment of this didactic concern in the context of Christian worship made the liturgy more an occasion of teaching about the faith, an essentially *mental* activity, than an occasion of the celebration of the faith which involved all dimensions of the human person, namely, in authentic sacramental worship.

The effect of this didactic concern imposed upon liturgical rites was far-reaching. Liturgical texts became the instruments through which right teaching might be effected. Liturgical rites came to bear the mark of the polemical debates which separated Christians, and thus became a sign of division rather than of unity in faith. To a great extent, this didactic distortion of the liturgy affected all churches that are characterized by liturgical forms of worship. Self-consciously non-liturgical Protestant churches were free to embrace wholeheartedly this understanding of the Sunday assembly, and there the sermon assumed a central role, set in the context of clearly secondary quasi-liturgical elements.

Within the liturgical traditions, the natural conservatism which holds tenaciously to a familiar ritual form thus offered a potential means by which an encompassing sacramental view of the liturgy might be recovered. The Liturgical Movement, whose origins are usually placed in the latter part of the nineteenth century, has had explicit impact in pastoral practice during recent years. As a whole, the heavy didacticism which had characterized a rationalist approach to Christian faith has now given way to an understanding of liturgy as the focus of the Church's proclamation of its faith in the signs of redemption.

It is in this perspective that the adage, "The law of prayer establishes the law of faith," emerges with dramatic significance in our time. The liturgy lifts up the faith in the common celebration of that faith by God's people gathered together, using words and signs in a corporate action which both expresses the faith into which all have been baptized, and at the same time nourishes that faith in each member of the assembly. In proclaiming the faith, the primary purpose of the rites is not a narrow didacticism. It is rather the formation of the common identity which all the baptized share, and which is the point of origin for their mission in the world as "other christs" through whom God's purposes are made tangible.

When we see the liturgy as a proclamation of Trinitarian faith, it is not as a doctrinal lecture which teaches *about* the faith but as a celebration of that faith into which all are baptized, and which is thus the foundation of the people's self-understanding in the world. When the eucharistic rite begins "Blessed be God: Father, Son, and Holy Spirit," this is not merely a convenient phrase to get things underway. It is a proclamation of what the rite is all about. The repertory of collects is also such a body of Trinitarin prayer in which, as we have seen in this study, a wide range of the Church's concerns is placed into a standard framework of praise and petition. The collects are thus more than prayers used to bring the entrance rite to a conclusion. Instead they are expressive of the essential nature of the entire action — prayer offered to God through the mediator Jesus Christ, whose Body in this place the assembly is, acting through the grace and power of the Holy Spirit. So the collect, with all the varied content of its many forms, is a microcosm of the Christian faith.

If we were to ask where that Trinitarian faith is most fully expressed in the liturgy, the probable response for many Christians would be in the recitation of the Creed. Given the didactic approach to liturgy which has dominated in recent centuries, that response is perhaps understandable, but requires correction. The Nicene Creed is a conciliar summary of the faith, intended as a test of orthodoxy and not at first for liturgical use. The liturgical creed is the Apostles' Creed, which developed in the context of Christian Initiation. The Nicene Creed did not find a place in the Western liturgy until the end of the eleventh century, and then at the close of centuries of intense conflict over doctrinal orthodoxy. In other words, the use of the Nicene Creed was connected with a didactic purpose.

If we look at the evolution of the eucharistic rite as a whole, the primary place in which the Trinitarian faith is most fully expressed is in the eucharistic prayer, the Great Thanksgiving. It is here that the Church's theology is prayed, proclaimed before the assembly which shares that faith. The various forms of the eucharistic prayer from the traditions of both East and West offer a rich array of images through which that faith is articulated, but it is evident from its substance and richness that, whatever its particular structure, the eucharistic prayer is *the* prayer of the entire action. It is the prayer in which the whole rite finds its foundation.

Christian worship is an act of Trinitarian faith. It is that faith which is articulated in the rite, and which requires such articulation as a sign of its being rooted in the Christian experience of God. It is interesting to note that the inclusion of the Nicene Creed in the eucharist developed only after the eucharistic prayer had come to be recited virtually in silence by the celebrant at the altar. Such silent recitation indicates a clericalization of the prayer — it pertained to the clergy and fell within the domain only of bishops and priests.[2] The sense of the prayer as the proclamation of the *Church*'s faith had become radically obscured, and the people reduced to silent observation of a remote ritual. The prayer itself was a clerical formula for producing the sacrament. One can see, in this perspective, the introduction of the Nicene Creed from a phenomenological point of view because it was the necessary articulation of the Church's faith within the liturgical context.

In terms of historical evolution, the Creed's role in the eucharist was as a surrogate for the primary but obscured role of the Prayer of Thanksgiving as the place in which Trinitarian faith received its fullest liturgical proclamation. The anomaly of the "silent canon" was, of course, removed from the eucharist by Thomas Cranmer in the first Book of Common Prayer (1549), where the rubric after the *Sanctus* indicates not only that the following words should be clearly proclaimed, but even that they might be sung. The rubric reads,

Theology Prayed

> *Then the Priest, turnyng hym to the Altar,*
> *shall saye or syng, playnly and distinctly,*
> *this prayer followyng.*[3]

Although Cranmer's rite reflected a continuation of the clerical domination of the liturgy, we find in this rubric a recovered awareness of the proclamatory character of the eucharistic prayer.

This concern for the role of the liturgy as the primary focus for the proclamation of the Church's faith is no peripheral matter. If the texts which we pray are indeed the faith which we share, then their proclamation in the midst of the assembly of baptized people has a formative impact upon the people gathered. The proclamation through word and sacrament becomes the foundation of the common memory shared by all believers of God's work of redemption in Christ and of the abiding presence of the Holy Spirit as the life-principle of the Church. What we acknowledge by faith in our corporate prayer is the basis of what we are becoming through the grace of God: what we pray is a manifestation of what we believe.

Although we have insisted upon the primacy of the role of the eucharistic prayer as the place at which the Trinitarian faith is proclaimed, the role of the collects is clearly complementary to that. The collects in their classical form are expressions of prayed faith in the Trinity. The shape of the collects in articulating that faith is parallel to the fundamental structure of the eucharistic prayer: prayer is addressed to God the Father as Creator and Source, upon the events of salvation history which are focused and summed up in the incarnate Christ, realized today through the present activity of the Holy Spirit.

It has often been noted in Anglican apologetical writings on the liturgy that most of the collects of the Prayer Book tradition were addressed to God the Father. However, it was not generally recognized that the rare exceptions, collects addressed to the Son, were *in that context* theological anomalies, which had inadvertently strayed from the great tradition of liturgical prayer. Anglican apologetical writings on the liturgy demonstrate a vague awareness that the directing of the collects to the Father is related to their fundamental use in the celebration of the eucharist. The following is a characteristic example of such explanations: "The reason why the Collects are nearly all addressed to the First Person of the Holy Trinity is that they were originally composed for use at Holy Communion, in which office we plead before the Father the merits and Passion of His Son, and naturally, therefore, address all our prayers directly to Him."[4]   Behind this rather literalized image of the mediatorial work of Christ lies the more fundamental issue. Christian corporate prayer exists only by virtue of the common Trinitarian faith which forms the Church, which brings the Church into being. That identity finds its essential expression in the eucharistic assembly in which the baptized are visibly constituted as the Body of Christ and participate in Christ's prayer and self-offering to God. In other words, the Church's identity as the Body of Christ is articulated in and through Trinitarian prayer: "The law of prayer establishes the law of faith."

This rooting of Trinitarian prayer in the inner being of the Church was so firmly sensed in the early centuries

[129]

of Christianity that any forms of prayer for public worship which did not conform to that model were associated with the heterodox teaching of heretical groups. It was really in confrontation with such groups that the Church was obliged to refine its understanding of the theology of its liturgical prayer. At the Synod of Hippo in 393, it was decreed that "at the altar, prayer shall always be addressed to the Father."[5] This regulation did not apply to the private prayer of Christians, who could also address prayer appropriately to the Son or the Holy Spirit as equally divine with the Father. The point was rather that the liturgical, public prayer of the Church had always been directed to the Father and that this was a determinative factor for the law of belief. Such prayer, when the Church was gathered for public worship, was the most adequate articulation of its faith.

Confrontation with the Arian heresy, which denied the full divinity of the Son, eventually led to the addressing of prayer to Christ as an assertion of his divinity. If he were not divine, such prayer would have been idolatrous. Thus prayer addressed to Christ was an expression of the denial of a heresy, but it eventually led to confusion in later forms of liturgical prayer where it is often unclear as to whether a prayer is addressed to the Father or the Son. This blurring of the Father and Son, with a consequent loss of a clear sense of Christ's mediatorial role, contributed to the emergence of the saints as mediators in popular piety, as I mentioned in the previous chapter.[6]

Eventually such prayer addressed to Christ was incorporated into the liturgical rites as the fundamental role of public worship as the expression of the Church's faith came to be obscured. Cranmer's collect for the Third Sunday of Advent, for example, was based upon an ambivalent Latin collect which seems to confuse the Father and the Son. The English version of the 1549 Prayer Book does not resolve this ambivalence:

> Lord, we beseche thee, geue eare to our prayers, and by thy gracious visitacion lighten the darkness of our hearte, by our Lorde Jesus Christe.

The words "thy gracious visitacion," coming on the threshold of Christmas, would seem to refer to the birth of Jesus, yet the collect concludes with "by our Lorde Jesus Christe," which suggests that the prayer is addressed to the Father. This collect was replaced in the 1662 Prayer Book with a prayer directed clearly to the Son:

> O Lord Iesu Christ, who at thy first coming didst send thy messenger to prepare thy way before thee . . . .

In the American Prayer Book of 1979, the collects are consistently addressed to God the Father. Yet, in the case of the collect for the Third Sunday of Advent, the form begins, "Stir up your power, O Lord, and with great might come among us." Given our recovery in recent years of the eschatological meaning of Advent, the petition that the Lord will "come among us" can be understood as a reference to the coming of the reign of God at the end of time. The near approach of Christmas, however, means that a certain ambivalence remains. The collect in the new Canadian Book of Alternative Services resolves the issue with a prayer which is clearly addressed to God the Father:

> God of power and mercy, you call us once again to celebrate the coming of your Son. Remove those things which hinder love of you, that when he comes, he may find us waiting in awe and wonder for him who lives and reigns with you and the Holy Spirit, one God, now and for ever.[7]

We see in this collect signs of the influence of the principles adopted by ICEL, in which two indicative sentences are used where Cranmer would have used a subordinate clause. Yet this is a good example of a more contemporary style that avoids the flatness which we observed in some early ICEL versions.

The calendar of the 1979 Prayer Book introduces a major feast of our Lord, the Visitation, which did not have propers in the 1928 version. The evolution of the collect for that feast is an interesting example of a recovery of the ancient tradition of liturgical prayer as always addressed to the Father. In the *Draft Proposed Book of Common Prayer*, the collect began:

> O incarnate God, whose virgin mother was blessed in bearing you . . . .

Quite evidently, this prayer is addressed to the incarnate Christ, not to the Father. In the final version of the

Prayer Book, the collect reads:

> Father in heaven, by your grace the virgin
> mother of your incarnate Son was blessed in
> bearing him, but still more blessed in
> keeping your word: Grant us who honor the
> exaltation of her lowliness to follow the
> example of her devotion to your will;
> through Jesus Christ our Lord . . . .

The essential content of the collect remains the same as in
the earlier version, but the shifting of the address to God
the Father indicates a conscious recovery of the great
tradition of Christian public prayer. This is not a matter
of theological hair-splitting. It is rather a question of the
integrity of Trinitarian faith as proclaimed in liturgical
prayer. Given the potentially formative impact of liturgical prayer in the light of the traditional axiom, "The law
of prayer constitutes the law of faith," the importance of
the role of the collect as expressing the intentionality of
the entire rite must not be underestimated. Jesus Christ,
the incarnate Son of God, is our mediator, our bridge to
the Father, the one *through* whom our prayer is
acceptable to the Father. It is important that our
liturgical forms not obscure that fundamental truth of
Christian faith.

The collect for the Visitation is theologically significant also in regard to our earlier discussion of the way
the collects for saints' days have been shaped within the
Anglican liturgical tradition. The collects for the feasts
associated with the Blessed Virgin Mary, as well as
collects in which images of her role in salvation history

[133]

are present, bring important theological concerns to the fore. It is significant that the Prayer Book lists three feasts which are certainly associated with the Virgin Mary in popular piety as 'Other Feasts of our Lord': the Presentation, the Annunciation, and the Visitation. From a theological point of view, this reflects a characteristic Anglican concern that the role of Mary always be seen in the context of her relation to Christ. Mary does not stand alone. Her role is as the bearer of the incarnate Son: Mary is the human instrument by whom God brought about the Incarnation.

This emphasis on Mary's relation to Christ is seen in a two-fold light in the collect for the Visitation: Mary's dignity, her "exaltation," rests both upon her role as "mother of your incarnate Son" and also upon her faithful obedience to the will of God. Mary is thus seen as a model for Christians who here pray "to follow the example of her devotion to your will."

The collect for the Presentation (February 2) does not make any explicit reference to Mary at all:

> Almighty and everlasting God, we humbly pray that, as your only-begotten Son was this day presented in the temple, so we may be presented to you with pure and clean hearts by Jesus Christ our Lord; who lives and reigns with you and the Holy Spirit, one God, now and for ever. *Amen.*

It is possible to hear in the reference to "pure and clean hearts" an echo of a collect for Christmas (3), which speaks of Christ's being "born of a pure virgin" and then

[134]

goes on to relate this to our rebirth "by adoption and grace" in baptism. It is useful to note that the feast of the Presentation, although occurring several weeks after Christmas, nevertheless falls within the framework of the images of that feast.

The collect for the feast of the Annunciation also clearly reflects the primacy of the Incarnation as the context for Mary's role in salvation history:

> Pour your grace into our hearts, O Lord, that we who have known the incarnation of your Son Jesus Christ, announced by an angel to the Virgin Mary, may by his cross and passion be brought to the glory of his resurrection; who lives and reigns with you, in the unity of the Holy Spirit, one God, now and for ever. *Amen.*

This primacy of the Incarnation as the context of Mary's role, so evident in the Annunciation collect, is also stated in the collect for Mary's own feast day (August 15), which is a new addition to the American Prayer Book calendar. The underlying image of the collect, without making a clear theological statement, is, of course, what is known as the Assumption in Roman Catholic piety and the Dormition in the Orthodox tradition. The essential point is that, after her death, the mother of Christ was taken to God:

> O God, you have taken to yourself the blessed Virgin Mary . . . .

But immediately the collect goes on to speak of her relation to Christ in the words, "mother of your incarnate Son," the same words used in the Visitation collect. Here again, in this collect, Mary is held up as a model for Christians, one in whom God has done what it is his will to do for all believers:

> Grant that we, who have been redeemed by
> his blood, may share with her the glory of
> your eternal kingdom . . . .

These collects of the Prayer Book are a significant theological source for our understanding of the role of the Blessed Virgin in Christian piety. She is above all else the historical instrument of the Incarnation, the woman and mother in whom God's redemptive purpose for the whole world was realized; she is the bearer of the incarnate God. Mary is also, by virtue of that, a model for all Christians. Her will was conformed to that of the Father and thus her life became an instrument of God. She is thus the model of faith, a faith which finds its fulfillment in the kingdom of God.

Such collects are a theological source. They are expressive both of Trinitarian faith and also of an understanding of holiness in the lives of the heroic men and women of the Christian tradition. In these examples, it is the faith of the Church's great tradition which is proclaimed both as the articulation of that faith and as a nurturing of that faith in the context of the Christian assembly. The faith proclaimed is the faith prayed, and that is the faith into which the community has been baptized. The prayer of the Church, especially in the principal Sunday assembly, is thus a primary sign of the unity of all Christians in a common faith which finds its highest expression in the praise of God.

Almighty God, you have knit together your elect in one communion and fellowship in the mystical body of your Son Christ our Lord: Give us grace so to follow your blessed saints in all virtuous and godly living, that we may come to those ineffable joys that you have prepared for those who truly love you; through Jesus Christ our Lord, who with you and the Holy Spirit lives and reigns, one God, in glory everlasting. *Amen.*

(Collect for All Saints)

Chapter 1: On Liturgical Prayer

[1]An analysis of this mentality is presented by Louis Bouyer in *Liturgical Piety* (University of Notre Dame, 1955), esp. pp. 1-22.

[2]An excellent discussion of the relation of different modes of prayer is presented by Gabe Huck in "Family and Individual Prayer" in *Liturgy 80* (special issue, July 1980).

[3]Balthasar Fischer, "The Common Prayer of Congregation and Family in the Ancient Church" in *Studia Liturgica* 10 (1974), pp. 117-118.

[4]See my essay, "Liturgical Creativity" in *Parish: A Place for Worship*, ed. Mark Searle (Collegeville, MN, 1981), esp. pp. 89-94.

Chapter 2: The Collect is Corporate Prayer

[1]*Constitution and Canons* (1985), Title III, Canon 15, Sec. 1 (a).

[2]A valuable survey of attitudes and practice in regard to the eucharist is presented by Nathan Mitchell in *Cult and Controversy* (New York, 1982).

[3]See Patrick W. Collins, *More Than Meets the Eye* (New York, 1983). The author is concerned about the failure of liturgical renewal to acknowledge the crucial role of the aesthetic dimensions of the liturgy.

[4]See Edmund Bishop, "The Genius of the Roman Rite" in *Liturgica Historica* (Oxford, 1918), pp. 1-19, esp. 13-16.

[5]Canon XX of the Canons of the Council of Nicaea, in *The Canons of the First Four General Councils of the Church*, ed. William Lambert (London, 1968), p. 25.

[6]See my essay, "The Liturgy on Great Occasions: Notes on Large-Scale Celebrations" in *Living Worship*, vol. 14, no. 2 (1978).

[7]See Ralph A. Keifer: "Liturgical Text as Primary Source For Eucharistic Theology" in *Worship*, vol. 51, no. 3 (1977), pp. 186-196.

[8]In the Eastern Orthodox rites, there is no variable prayer which corresponds to the Western collect. In the Byzantine rite, for example, there is a prayer immediately prior to the readings that is related to the "minor entrance" of the book, and which is placed within a context of repetition of the *Trisagion* by the choir.

[9]Joseph Jungmann, *The Mass of the Roman Rite: Its Origins and Development* (New York, 1950), 1:372-375 (hereafter cited as Jungmann, *Roman Rite*).

[10]See Evelyn Underhill: "The constantly repeated *Oremus* of the Latin service books, the elaborate biddings in the Gallican and other early rites, and the summing up of the people's litany by the priest in the liturgy of the Orthodox Church, are there to remind us of the truly corporate function of the Collect; really a device for securing the active participation of the people in the whole spiritual movement of worship, gathering up and giving detailed and explicit utterance to their secret prayer . . . . The collect or prayer of the leader, then, is truly congregational in the deeper if not in the obvious sense." *Worship* (New York, 1936), pp. 109-110.

[11]See Marion J. Hatchett, *Commentary on the American Prayer Book* (New York, 1980), p. 101.

[12]See Jungmann's discussion of Amalarius' comments on the Roman rite in 830 A.D. *Roman·Rite*, 1:385-386.

Chapter 3: *Structuring the Community's Prayer*

[1]"There can hardly be any doubt that the oration and the *Kyrie* belong together . . . . The ancient Church was conscious of the fact that the litany demanded a concluding prayer by the priest." Compare this with: "[the choir sings] an entrance psalm, exactly as they afterwards sing the offertory psalm and the communion psalm. This external event is concluded with a prayer, as is proper in an assembly gathered for worship." Jungmann, *Roman Rite*, 1:265-266. G. G. Willis notes that the introit psalm was part of the structure of the entrance rite before an

entrance litany was introduced, not to mention its vestigial *Kyrie.* (*Further Essays in the Early Roman Liturgy*, pp. 108-109.)

[2]*First Apology*, Ch. 67:3-5; in *The Eucharist of the Early Christians* (New York, 1978), p. 73.

[3]*The Treatise on the Apostolic Tradition of St Hippolytus of Rome*, ed. Gregory Dix, rev. Henry Chadwick (London, 1968). In the material for both the baptismal and ordination rites, no opening prayer is indicated.

[4]Christine Mohrmann suggests that the process was completed between 360-382. See *Liturgical Latin: Its Origins and Character* (London, 1959), p. 50.

[5]See H. K. Hughes' discussion of this question in "*The Opening Prayers of 'The Sacramentary': A Structural Study of the Prayers of the Easter Cycle.*" (Ph.D. dissertation, Notre Dame, Department of Theology, 1980.) Ann Arbor, MI: University Microfilms, 1981, pp. 13-16.

[6]*Sacramentarium Veronense*, ed. L. C. Mohlberg; Rerum Ecclesiasticarum Documenta, Fontes I (Rome, 1956), item 1239, p. 157.

[7]"The Solemn Prayers of Good Friday" in *Essays in Early Roman Liturgy* (London, 1964), pp. 1-48, esp. 3-10.

[8]It is from the end of the fourth century that intercessory prayers began to appear within the context of The

Great Thanksgiving. Jungmann comments that "the core of the intercessory prayer in the Roman liturgy as well as in others, was transferred to the inner sanctuary of the eucharistic prayer." *Roman Rite*, 2:152. The implications of this observation are far-reaching. The eucharistic prayer was coming to be viewed as the sacred domain of the clergy, and hence a more effective context for intercession. Such a view is indicative of the radical break which was thus emerging between the respective roles of clergy and laity in the liturgical assembly.

[9]This is a primary example of what is known as "Baumstark's Law": "Primitive conditions are maintained with greater tenacity in the more sacred seasons of the Liturgical Year." (Anton Baumstark: *Comparative Liturgy*. London, 1958, p. 27.)

[10]See T. Klauser, *A Short History of the Western Liturgy* (Oxford, 1979), p. 102.

[11]*The Shape of the Liturgy*, pp. 446-447.

[12]Willis, *op. cit.*, pp. 110-111.

[13]*Eucharistic Liturgies of Edward VI: A Text for Students*, ed. Colin Buchanan (Grove Liturgical Studies, 1983), pp. 7-8.

[14]The *Gloria in excelsis* has been characterized as a type of popular hymn modelled on the psalms. If that view is correct, the *Gloria* is rather like a festive alternative to the customary entrance psalm of the classical Western rite,

and would thus be appropriately used as an element in the entrance rite.

[15]See Ralph A. Keifer, "Our Cluttered Vestibule: The Unreformed Entrance Rite" in *Worship*, vol 48, no. 5 (1974), pp. 270-277.

[16]See Hans-Ludwig Kulp, "Das Gemeindegebet in christlichen Gottesdienst" in *Leiturgia* (Kassel, 1955), 2:411-412.

[17]*A Rational Illustration of the Book of Common Prayer of the Church of England* (Oxford, 1946), p. 135.

Chapter 4: Using Words to Pray

[1]Peter E. Fink, "Three Languages of Christian Sacraments" in *Worship*, vol. 52, no. 6 (1978), pp. 561-575.

[2]Ibid., p. 562.

[3]C. S. Lewis, *God in the Dock: Essays in Theology and Ethics*, ed. W. Hooper (Grand Rapids, 1970), p. 231.

[4]Robert Speaight, "Liturgy and Language" in *Theology*, vol. 74, no. 616 (October 1971), p. 456.

[5]See Richard Toporoski, "The Language of Worship" in *Worship*, vol. 52, no. 6 (1978), pp. 489-508. It should be noted that this entire issue of *Worship* was devoted to

liturgical language and is a valuable resource on the subject.

[6]Christine Mohrmann, *Liturgical Latin: Its Origin and Character* (London, 1959), p. 66; see also pp. 65-68.

[7]*The Church Year*, Prayer Book Studies 19, III. The Proper (New York, 1970), p. 40.

[8]Ibid., p. 41.

[9]Stella Brook, *The Language of The Book of Common Prayer* (London, 1965), p. 126.

[10]See Richard Toporoski, "The Language of Worship" in *Worship*, vol. 52, no. 6 (1978), p. 490. (It should be noted that the Roman Missal in English, which is the currently authorized form of the ICEL versions, is now in a gradual process of revision which will be completed in the early 1990s. It is understood that a new approach to the linguistic style of the collects is leading to significant differences from those which were authorized in 1973.)

[11]Leonel L. Mitchell, "The Collects of the Proposed Book of Common Prayer" in *Worship*, vol. 52, no. 2 (1978), pp. 141-142.

[12]Massey H. Shepherd, Jr., *The Oxford American Prayer Book Commentary* (New York, 1950, p. 134.

[13]Marion J. Hatchett, *Commentary on the American Prayer Book* (New York, 1980), pp. 163-216.

¹⁴See Jean Deshusses, *Le Sacramentaire Grégorien*, vol. 1 (Fribourg, 1971), item 423, p. 200. (See Hatchett, p. 14.)

¹⁵*Liber Sacramentorum Romanae Aeclesiae Ordinis Anni Circuli*, ed. L. C. Mohlberg; Rerum Ecclesiasticarum Documenta, Fontes IV (Rome, 1960), item 638, p. 100.

¹⁶Hatchett, p. 184.

¹⁷Ibid., p. 172.

¹⁸See Mohlberg, item 1080, p. 165.

¹⁹Jeremy Taylor, "An Apology for Authorized and Set Forms of Liturgy" in *Anglicanism*, More and Cross, eds. (Milwaukee, 1935), p. 177.

²⁰See *Lesser Feasts and Fasts*, 3d ed. (New York, 1980), pp. iv-vi.

²¹August 13, *LFF*, p. 293; April 3, *LFF*, p. 193. It is interesting to note that the Church of England has not made such allusions in its collects for lesser saints' days: cf. *The Child of Witnesses* (London, 1982), p. 134.

²²February 15, *LFF*, p. 147. (Italics added.)

²³Authorized by the General Convention, 1985. (Italics added.)

Chapter 5: Theology Prayed

[1]See Geoffrey Wainwright, *Doxology* (New York, 1980), pp. 218-283. Related material by other authors may be found in *Worship*, vol. 57, no. 4 (July 1983), pp. 309-332. Cf. also Aidan Kavanagh, *On Liturgical Theology* (New York, 1984), esp. pp. 73-121.

[2]See A. G. Martimort, *The Church at Prayer: The Eucharist* (New York, 1973), pp. 139-140.

[3]*The First and Second Prayer-Books of King Edward the Sixth* (London, no date), p. 221.

[4]Evan Daniel, *The Prayer Book, Its History, Language, and Contents* (London, 1905), p. 223.

[5]See C. Vagaggini, *Theological Dimensions of the Liturgy* (Collegeville, MN, 1976), p. 210.

[6]The major study of this subject is Joseph Jungmann's *The Place of Christ in Liturgical Prayer* (London, 1965). For a recent reconsideration of the issue, see Albert Gerhards, "Prière addressée à Dieu ou au Christ?" in *Liturgie, Spiritualité, Cultures*, ed. A. M. Triacca and A. Pistoia (Rome, 1982), pp. 101-114.

[7]*The Book of Alternative Services of the Anglican Church of Canada* (Toronto, 1985), p. 270.

SUGGESTIONS FOR FURTHER READING

William Bright, *Ancient Collects and Other Prayers* (Oxford, 1962).

Patrick W. Collins, *More Than Meets the Eye* (New York, 1983).

Marion J. Hatchett, *Commentary on the American Prayer Book* (New York, 1980).

H. K. Hughes, R.S.C.J., "*The Opening Prayers of 'The Sacramentary': A Structural Study of the Prayers of the Easter Cycle.*" (Ph.D. dissertation, Notre Dame, Department of Theology, 1980. Ann Arbor, MI: University Microfilms, 1981.)

Joseph Jungmann, S.J., *The Place of Christ in Liturgical Prayer* (Staten Island,NY, 1964).

John Wallace Suter, Jr., *The Book of English Collects* (New York, 1940).

G. G. Willis, *Further Essays in Early Roman Liturgy* (London, 1968), pp. 89-131.